FULLNESS OF TIME

FULLNESS OF TIME
SHORT STORIES OF WOMEN AND AGING

Martha Whitmore Hickman

UPPER ROOM BOOKS

Nashville

FULLNESS OF TIME

No part of this book may be reproduced in any manner whatsoever without written permission of the publisher except in brief quotations embodied in critical articles or reviews. For information address The Upper Room, 1908 Grand Avenue, P.O. Box 189, Nashville, TN 37202.

Unless otherwise identified, Scripture quotations are from the Today's English Version Bible - Old Testament: Copyright © American Bible Society 1976; New Testament: Copyright © American Bible Society 1966, 1971, 1976. Used by permission.

Scripture quotations designated RSV are from the Revised Standard Version Bible, copyright © 1946, 1952, 1971 by the Division of Christian Education of the National Council of Churches of Christ in the U.S.A. Used by permission.

Excerpt from the hymn "Lift Every Voice and Sing" (James Weldon Johnson, J. Rosamond Johnson). Used by permission of Edward B. Marks Music Co. and Hal Leonard Publishing Company.

"The Last Hour" originally appeared in *Weavings: A Journal of the Christian Spiritual Life*, Volume IV, Number 3 (May/June 1989), © 1989 by The Upper Room.

Cover Illustration: David Klein
Cover Design: C. J. Helms
Book Design: Richard Cook
Interior Illustration: Richard Cook
First Printing: October 1990 (10)
Library of Congress Catalog Card Number: 90-70326
ISBN 0-8358-0620-0

Printed in the United States of America

To our Mothers
and our Grandmothers—
    Ruth, Martha, Carrie
    Mayme, Edith, Bess
with love and gratitude

CONTENTS

INTRODUCTION

The stories we tell one another are among our strongest ways of drawing close, of sharing our lives. The stories grandparents tell about what it was like when they were young and our eagerness to hear from those we love the stories of their growing up attest to our natural hunger for stories as ways of knowing who we are, who each other is. There is a way in which we keep ourselves alive by stories—not as literally as Scheherazade in *Arabian Nights' Entertainments*, or *The Thousand and One Nights*, who put off her death by extending her story a night at a time—but as a way of keeping our lives vivid, meaningful, present before our very eyes.

Stories express, in their symbols and leaps of imagination, dimensions of life and experience which can't be arrived at in the abstract terms of theory and idea. Jesus conveyed his teaching through stories: "Once there was a man who went out early in the morning to hire some men to work in his vineyard" (Matt. 20:1). . . . "Suppose a woman who has ten silver coins loses one of them—what does she do?" (Luke 15:8).

Down through the years writers have conveyed messages of insight, faith, and love through fiction. We think of Tolstoy's story "Where Love Is, There God Is Also" in which Martin the cobbler entertains the Lord unaware in the person of an old soldier, a hungry woman with her baby, and a boy stealing an apple. The fiction of contemporary writers like John Updike, Flannery O'Connor, Larry Woiwode, Nancy Willard often explores and illuminates issues of faith.

The stories in this book are stories on aging, on women and aging—though there are men in the stories, too. It is no news by now that the median age in the U.S. grows older year by year. Older people have the most stories to tell, the most memories to share, and perhaps the most need to rest in stories of aging and its particular redemptions. They are in some ways both subject and audience for this book.

But not they alone. These stories will, I hope, help those who love and care for older people—and surely that includes most of us!—know how it feels to move in the realm of older persons, and with such knowledge act with more compassion, confidence, and understanding.

And all of us, as we face our own launching into senior years, can use all the help we can get—not only in the role models we know and cherish but in stories of how other people have met some of the changes and challenges of aging:

What helps a person build a home within so secure that no turn of adversity or ill health can make it fall?

What happens to relationships with family and friends as we grow older?

What of the dreams we have cherished that come to look quite different as the time to accomplish them grows short?

What of the homes we live in as our life circumstances change? What are the best things to take with us if we move? A picture? A book? A piece of furniture? A recipe? Surely, memories and the appetite for new friends and new adventures.

So these stories deal with some of the common adventures of growing old—the move to a retirement home and the relinquishment of illusions, and sometimes of old griefs and grudges in favor of more satisfying realities. Stories of giving up special tasks, of cherishing independence, of finding a grandchild, of the emergence through the distillations of age and adversity of a kind of purified self. Stories of the summoning of resources, of courage, of acceptance of frailty as well as the knowledge that in terms of adventure—even of new romance—it's not over till it's over. And when it's over, the faith that something wonderful is beginning!

One more word. These stories were conceived in faith, though the language of faith is often only implied—something in their circumstance, the response of their characters to life events. Each story is also preceded by a brief scripture selection. The stories are in no way "translations" of the scriptural passages; rather, story and scripture are illuminations of one another. It has been said that a saint is one through whom the light shines. May the light shine through these stories too.

SHORT STORIES OF WOMEN AND AGING

I will give you peace in your land, and you can sleep without being afraid of anyone. . . . I will live among you in my sacred Tent, and I will never turn away from you. I will be with you; I will be your God, and you will be my people.

Leviticus 26:6, 11-12

THE LAST HOUR

You sit here, Mother." Ginny moved the most comfortable lawn chair into the shade and patted the green and white webbing. "You can watch the whole yard sale from here."

"I might be needed, too," she said. "People may want to know things you don't know"—she caught Ginny's look of impatience—"just about things that go back before you were born."

Ginny nodded. "I guess." She hurried to the card table holding the china—the Haviland plates, the gold-embossed Nippon cups and saucers—rearranged a few cups, then came back. "We've priced things high to start," she said. "If no one buys them, we'll reduce everything about three o'clock, for the last hour."

The phrase "the last hour" caught under Lydia's breast bone. How could Ginny speak of it like that? It should be whispered—the prospect of the close of this sale—the words somehow shrouded in velvet.

She picked up the ivory fan, spread its carved fingers out to a half circle, and fanned herself.

"It'll be hot here before long, when the sun gets around," she said. She'd never been able to stand the heat—even less able since the angina—her heart always on the edge of racing.

"Well, we'll move the chair then, dear. We'll keep you safe, don't worry."

There was, that time, a touch of compassion in her daughter's voice. How could she tell her, safe means nothing to me now? Safe is fifty years ago when your father and I were young and you children were running in ditches, swimming in strong currents, and we worried about polio every summer. Safe is my mother and I having tea on the back veranda when I went to visit and took you with me—a baby in a basket lying on the porch. Since your father died, safe is only where you are. Safe is what we do not speak of.

A long black car pulled up to the edge of the lawn. A man in a pin-striped suit stepped out onto the grass. He wore a flat straw hat which he doffed as he came close. He said to Lydia, "I know your sale doesn't start for a while. Is it all right if I look around?"

"No," she said. "We're not selling anything ahead of time. We advertised nine o'clock. It wouldn't be fair to the other customers to begin earlier."

The man looked at Ginny, his eyebrows raised in a question. "Any chance, Ma'am?"

Ginny smiled. Lydia had seen that smile before. She hated it. It meant Ginny was trying to pass something off, to pretend something was inconsequential. "I think it's all right, Mother." Ginny gestured toward the clutter of objects on tables and grass. "We have so much to get rid of. We might as well let this gentleman see if there's anything he's interested in."

She acquiesced—not out of conviction, but because she was powerless. And because the whole thing grieved her—this disposition of the objects of her life.

It wasn't the first time. Ten years ago, when Will died and she'd moved from the big house in Northampton to New Paltz to be near Ginny, she'd reduced her household goods—given to Ginny and Art what they could use, sold some things, given some to the Salvation Army. But that time she felt she'd retained some footing in the world. She'd given Will's World War I uniform to the town museum. Later, visiting in Northampton, she'd gone down to see it, in the room off the library. It was in a glass case. "Gift of Mrs. William Randall," the card said. It pleased her. Passing back through the children's reading room with the low tables, the crayon drawings on the corkboard—prizes in some school art contest— she had looked at the children—fingers twisting their hair around their ears, glasses sliding down noses, chairs askew. When they studied history, they could go and look at Will's uniform.

She'd brought with her only the favorite things—the highboy, the alabaster lamp with the parchment shade that had always sat on the cherry table. How many evenings had the children done their homework by its light? Her mother's Bavarian teapot. The pewter bread tray the Sunday school class had given her one Christmas. "I am the bread of life," it said in high squared letters on the rim. The hand-carved walnut bed she and Will had slept in their entire married life.

The bed, dismantled, leaned against the white clapboard wall of the porch.

In the Home, where she was going, she couldn't use the bed—it was too big. "We use only single beds here, Mrs. Randall."

It was an affront. "Don't you ever have couples here?" she asked the superintendent, a tall, erect woman in a nurse's uniform, her hair piled in gray sculptured curls on her head. She was probably embarrassing Ginny, but she didn't care.

"Occasionally we do, but with elderly people we find they sleep better in a bed by themselves."

The superintendent wore no wedding ring. It didn't prove anything. Maybe she was married, or had a string of lovers, or a steady man. But didn't she know how well you slept if you could feel the one you loved beside you?

A Miss Courtney, a plump woman with bright brown eyes, who was an aide at Happy Acres (she couldn't abide that name—it sounded like cows being put out to pasture) was working at a glass medicine case nearby when this conversation was going on. She'd come close to Lydia as she and Ginny walked down the corridor, "You want a double bed, sweetheart, we'll push them together. You just see me."

"My father passed away ten years ago," Ginny said. "My mother will be coming here by herself."

"So?" Miss Courtney said. "It doesn't mean she'll stay by herself. We have eligible men here, you know."

The thought of eligible men made Lydia's stomach retract. It was too late for her to be sharing intimacies with anyone new. A couple of bags of bones cranking around over each other. If Will was here it would be different—they had watched the changes in each other benevolently, almost as though they were one body, loved, growing older. But a new person, with new knees and rump and sagging shoulders? No.

The man in the black car had come and gone, taking a set of bookshelves with him. Ginny came back to stand beside her.

"I don't see what's the hurry," Lydia said. "We should have waited until nine."

"Oh, Mother." Ginny pursed her lips and walked away, started redistributing old urns and small tables to fill in the space.

She sighed, sounding theatrical even to herself.

It wasn't the yard sale that made her and Ginny so edgy with each other. It was that she was moving to a Home. She knew it was the best solution. Even this small house was too much for her to keep up. She didn't want to move in with Ginny and Art, who had, somewhat halfheartedly, invited her. They both worked all day, and with the angina like it was she needed to be where she could get help right away. Besides, they needed their independence. And so did she. They could visit each other, after all. They'd be in the same town.

But even after she'd been accepted at Happy Acres, she delayed going until she could decide what to do with the things. She would like to have passed the choicest items on to Ginny. But Ginny's life was much too busy for crystal goblets and embroidered pillowcases.

They decided on the yard sale. After that, she would go—she'd asked Happy Acres to send Miss Courtney to pick her up. Art could take over most of her few things the day before.

She'd had words with Ginny about that, too. "Mother, it'll look very strange—us being right here, if you don't let us take you. Why not stay overnight? We can take you the next morning."

"Thank you, but no. Going is going. Once my things are sold I want to get there. Just me at first." Was it pride only that made her want to enter the place by herself? Or fear? Fine if Ginny came the next day. But it would just compound the emotional weight if she were to walk into Happy Acres on Ginny's arm. Too much between them. Better to go with a stranger, or someone she hardly knew. Miss Courtney.

By nine o'clock the first groups had come and by nine-thirty the lawn was crowded. People moved from table to table like grazing cattle. Her iron cookware went right away. She watched a succession of people pick up her food mill, set it down, lift the top bowl from the nest of cream and blue crockery, turn it over to read the markings, set it down. People moved by her, sometimes nodding perfunctorily, sometimes looking past her as though she weren't there at all. She watched them take their purchases to Ginny, pay for them, and wander off.

At eleven her neighbor, Mattie, came over. "Oh, I hate to see you go," Mattie said, furtively scanning the dwindling supply of household goods. She picked up a ceramic dish for deviled eggs. "I didn't know you had this. It'll be nice for summer picnics." Her voice had an edge of mourning, as though she must temper her pleasure in finding the plate out of regard for Lydia, who would be losing it and, far worse, moving to a Home.

People climbed on and off the porch. One by one the items went—the mahogany gate-legged table, the Kerman rug draped over the loveseat and now rolled up for carrying. She watched the back of a rotund man as he walked off with it—a long roll drooping over his shoulder. She was glad not to see his face. It had been one of her favorite possessions, and she was sure the man wasn't worthy of it. She didn't even see the bed go.

The heat of the sun overhead told her it must be at least noon. She'd left her watch inside. Ginny brought out sandwiches and iced tea. "It's after one o'clock, Mother. I think things are going well, don't you?"

"Is it that late?" she said in a sudden panic. "I guess so. Yes. Thank you." She took the small tray of sandwiches and tea and set it on a nearby table. "I'll just put it here." Ginny went back to her post.

Lydia felt sick at her stomach. One-thirty? Soon it would be two. Then three. Then four. Everything was going. Her eyes lit on the bread tray. "I am the bread of life," and, on the other side, "Man does not live by bread alone." How could she have thought to give that up? With a quick gesture she swept it off the table and into the carryall she'd brought out to hold her day's provender— glasses case, a sweater, a book in the event that things got slow.

She felt better, as though she had rescued someone from drowning. By four there would be nothing left. Nothing except empty tables, and money in the box, and her suitcase inside the door ready to go.

These people pawing over her things—by what right were they doing it? And where was Will? And how had she ever come to this place in her life? And how could she stand it when the car drove up and she had to walk across this lawn? There was Ginny over there, taking in the money, talking to folks as though it were any old day. At that moment Ginny, too, looked up, and their eyes met. Was it possible there was a look of panic in her daughter's eyes, too? She hoped it was so. Not that she wanted Ginny sad. But she wanted something to mark the occasion, how . . . momentous it was.

The crowds were suddenly thick again around the tables. She watched them fingering the lace shawls. At the far end of the table she saw a hand lift the cross-stitched linen tablecloth and napkins from Austria—beautiful, but needed ironing. Of late years she'd hardly used them at all. The Madeira placemats the same. Not that she had stooped to plastic. But woven mats you could hang to dry. Or an occasional cotton and polyester blend. Ginny had no use for these linens, either. It was a shame.

Looking down at the table again, she saw the luncheon set was gone. And then, shifting her glance to Ginny—she did look tired, standing over there all day—she saw a dark-haired woman leaning toward her, talking. She was holding the luncheon set in her hand. They'd put a price of $15 on it, which was ridiculous—you'd pay a hundred for it in a fine linen shop. She'd said that to Ginny, too. "But this isn't a linen shop, Mother. We've got to move things. They only go if they're cheap."

"Well, all right, but put me far from the money exchanges. I don't want to see that part of it."

Now Ginny was pointing over this way. Lydia saw the dark-haired woman start toward her, the luncheon set a bulky roll in her hand.

"Uh-oh, she's going to want it for nothing," she muttered, and clasped her hands on the angular incline of her knees and prepared to defend the small charge for such a valuable item.

The woman came close and leaned toward her over the chair. "That lady over there says this was yours."

Lydia nodded yes and waited for the question. But instead the woman's face broke into a smile. "It's beautiful," she said softly. "We had one when I was a tiny girl, in Poland. My mother did the work herself." She unfolded the roll slightly, fingered the bright stitching.

"And it got spoiled?" Lydia guessed. "Or you gave it away and wished you hadn't?"

The woman looked up. "I don't know what happened to it," she said. "I was sent away for safety." She hesitated, and her voice faltered but not much, as though she had said it too many times to trip on it now. "I never saw any of them again."

"Oh, my. Please," Lydia said, her heart plummeting. "Oh," she said again, looking back and forth from the linen set to the woman's face. "Please take this one. I'm so glad you have it."

"Oh, I mean to pay for it," the woman said. "I just wanted to tell you how much it means to me."

"No, please." Lydia took her hand. "I want you to have it. It's been . . . it's been looking for a home."

The woman's eyes glistened. "Oh, thank you." She nodded again and, clutching the rolled linen against her ample bosom, hurried across the grass.

Lydia watched her go, and some of the legacy of fine handwork she would have given Ginny if Ginny cared she bestowed again, almost with a royal gesture, upon the departing woman.

She sat back. She felt better, there was no denying it. As though the old tablecloth had taken wing, like a magic carpet, and lifted her above all mundane things, above all sadness even. "Bless you," she said, and watched the woman step into a shabby car and drive away, just a little too fast, as though the energy of delight added some unforeseen extra weight to her foot on the gas pedal.

Then she picked up the carryall from under her chair, set it firmly on her lap, and sat back to wait for Miss Courtney.

I have asked the Lord for one thing;
   one thing only do I want:
to live in the Lord's house all my life,
   to marvel there at his goodness,
   and to ask for his guidance.
In times of trouble he will shelter me;
   he will keep me safe in his Temple.

Psalm 27:4-5

THE POTATO MASHER

Everyone knew the potato masher couldn't last forever. Few of the church people remembered a time when it hadn't stood there in the kitchen—for most of the year a hovering, shrouded presence at the far end of the stainless steel counter, its scarred metal base splaying out beneath the muslin cover, like shoes sticking out from under a choir robe or a ministerial gown.

But once a year, for the annual Turkey Dinner and Bazaar that the women of the church put on, the potato masher was unveiled and its splendid steel-looped paddle churned its way around the heavy steel bowl, turning fifty pounds of boiled potatoes at a time, along with measured amounts of cooking water, hot milk, melted butter, and salt, into a creamy malleable mass of potato, to be dished out, along with turkey, stuffing, green beans, and a little fluted paper cup of cranberry, onto the plates of the eager diners who had come to the chief fund-raising event for which the women were justifiably famous.

Maddy Edwards always ran the potato masher. The machine was really an all-purpose mixer, but since it was used almost exclusively for mashing potatoes that was how they always referred to it.

No one knew how it came to be Maddy's domain. Even those who were close to her in age—she was seventy-two—didn't remember a time when Maddy hadn't done that particular job. During the years when she had been in charge of the whole dinner and bazaar, she had still managed to run the masher. "All right, start carving," she would say to the several husbands who loyally turned up each year, carving sets in hand, to dismember the birds their wives had cooked at home and brought, steaming in their roasting pans, to the church in the late afternoon. "Put the white meat and dark in separate piles," she'd remind them, "so we get some of each on every plate." She would stop by the huge black stove to check on the gravy stirrers and the warmers of the canned beans (until later, when they switched to frozen), the cutters-up of giblets, working at their cutting boards. Then she'd say, "I'll do the potatoes." The pies were already cut—wedges of mince and pumpkin lined up on plates on the tables of the nearest Sunday school room.

Maddy had never been president of the Women's Society, or sung in the choir, or been on any of the governing boards of the church. She had taught Sunday school when her children were young and the whole family went—Harold to the men's class, the children to their particular age group, Maddy to the women's class until she was recruited for teaching. For a few years she had taught the kindergarten class, and then for a few more she had taught the junior high girls. Occasionally she would review a chapter in the mission study book, and she took her turn doing the refreshments for the circle meeting and the general meeting. But, everyone agreed, Maddy had always done a bang-up job with the Turkey Dinner and Bazaar. "That's something I can do for the church," she would say modestly when, at each December meeting, the treasurer announced a handsome sum garnered from the annual Turkey Dinner and Bazaar, asked Maddy to stand, and thanked her for her excellent work.

"It's all of us working together," she'd say, in response to their applause, and she would sit down, content.

Then she gave up chairing the bazaar part of it, though she was still in charge of the dinner. Elsa Tomlinson took over the bazaar. Elsa was better at handwork and she got some of the young people involved. She even got Maddy's 15-year-old daughter, Susan who was balking at going to Sunday school and appeared to be growing generally indifferent to the church, to operate the fishbowl. To aid the cause and encourage Susan, Maddy contributed some of her best costume jewelry, and was secretly delighted when Jeffie, ten, spent fifty cents of his allowance on the fishbowl and hooked up her fake emerald earrings—which he gave to her for Christmas, not realizing they were hers.

Her children grown, she gave up teaching Sunday school. She and Harold liked to have a leisurely reading of the Sunday paper before church, so they often skipped Sunday school altogether. But she kept being in charge of the annual Turkey Dinner—she could manage that. When Harold died, she was glad to have that project to occupy herself—though when the men lined up to do the carving she felt a sudden renewed jab of pain. No Harold.

Then her arthritis worsened, and she gave up managing the dinner—it was just too much and it was getting harder and harder to get people to help. So many of the young women worked. It was all they could do to attend their once-a-month evening circle meeting and the general meeting of the women—now also held, out of deference to them, in the evening. "But I'll still do the potatoes," Maddy said.

It was September, and the first business of the meeting was planning for the Turkey Dinner and Bazaar. Ruth Warren began to distribute sign-up sheets—who would volunteer to set tables, bake pies, cook the turkeys, help with cleanup? One of the young women, her short, dark hair in an elegant swirl around her head, raised a hand from the back row. "I know the Turkey Dinner has been a tradition," she said. "But frankly, maybe its time has passed. I'd much rather increase my contribution—" She broke off and lowered her hand, her polished fingernails and gleaming gold bracelet catching the light.

For a moment there was silence. The young women on either side of the speaker nodded as though in agreement. One of them leaned over and whispered something in her ear. Then Ruth said, her voice a trifle apologetic, "Thank you, Stacey. But some of us enjoy the fellowship."

A buzz broke out in the back row. Lark Romelade, an intern in a local accounting firm, said, "Some of us have plenty of fellowship at work. What I long for . . ." she paused as though to accentuate the depth of her longing, "is more time with my family." Again the back-row heads nodded.

Maddy, seated in the second row, felt as tense as that time she had begun her stint on jury duty. Ruth smiled deferentially at the row of young women. "We talked about this at the executive board meeting," she said. "We know you folks can't help much with the dinner and bazaar. But it's meant a lot to the church, and some of us want to keep it going for a while. Just do what you can—and we'll welcome those contributions."

There was a general wave of relieved laughter, and when the sign-up sheet got to Maddy she wrote, "Two pies—pumpkin. Help with dinner—potatoes," and passed the sheet along the row—her tension over the whole issue moving away from her as the piece of paper traveled along the laps to her left.

There were so many things changing. Sometimes it made her feel almost dizzy, or at least made her wonder what her place was in the world anymore. Her children were all grown and moved to distant parts of the country. They came home from time to time. Each summer she had the grandchildren for a week or so, and it seemed like old times. They looked through the photo albums; she took them on picnics to the park and to the zoo. She made her special maple custard that her children had always loved. But then they would all be gone, and she would be lonesome all over again.

And now the church, that bulwark of stability while she and Harold were raising the children, that place that had given her spirit a home when Harold died, where she'd made her closest friends among the women—that too was changing. They even had a young woman minister—a nice enough person but she'd probably never mashed a potato in her life. Maddy could not look at her without feeling some silent self-reproach—the young woman so smart, with degrees, and traveling all over the country and calling God Mother. And now those young women agitating to drop the Turkey Dinner and Bazaar. Well, thank goodness, they hadn't succeeded this time.

Two weeks before the dinner, the committee met in the church kitchen to wash the dishes and silverware and cooking equipment in preparation for the big day.

Maddy had not meant to make a big thing of it, but she did have special feelings for that potato masher—all the years she had operated it through one turkey dinner after another. It wasn't easy to make it go, old and temperamental as it was. But *she* could—she could make it go. She had always prided herself on having a way with electrical equipment. "I might have been an engineer," she said to Harold at home one day when, noticing a suspicious falter in the sweeper's motor, he had tried to fix it and been unable to. "I'd better take this to the shop," he said.

"Wait a minute." She had turned it over and found a partial tear in the belt. "Here's what's making the noise," she showed him. She had an extra belt, and she put it on, stretching it with the bowl of a spoon to get it over the spindle. "There. I could have been an engineer," she said. He nodded, impressed with her skill. "I'm sure you could have," he said. That was one thing about Harold— he was very free with his praise. But now he was gone, and there was no one to tell her she'd done a good job—about anything. Except the grandchildren, who loved her cooking and the versions of "Chopsticks" she taught them to play on the piano, thumping in triads up and down the black keys.

"That's good, Grandma!" they would say and immediately try it out themselves.

So maybe she did care inordinately that she and she alone ran the potato masher.

Anyway, when Barbara Allison had the big sink full of warm suds and said, "Here, pass me the potato masher bowl and paddle. I'll wash them, too," Maddy had rushed over before Tootie Wilkins could turn the release button or disengage the paddle and said, "Here, I'll do it." Tootie stepped back to make way for her, and she dislodged paddle and bowl and brought them to Barbara, who stood at the sink, her dripping hands suspended over the soapy water. It was then she heard Ruth mutter to Tootie, "Maddy thinks nobody else can work the potato masher." Tootie, bless her heart, answered, "Well, maybe they can't. It looks pretty tricky to me."

"Oh, it's not complicated," Maddy had said, trying to pass it off. But it was. And getting more and more temperamental every year. You had to know how to put the paddle in, with that little knob fitting into the groove on the right of the housing. Then you had to start the machine real slow, like a car on an icy road. And some-times you had to press your hand on the side of the motor and lean against it, or it just wouldn't go.

Years ago, they had talked of having it overhauled. It had, of course, long since outrun its warranty. In fact, the company that made it had gone out of business, and no one had seen an instruction booklet for years. They had checked on replacement costs. A new potato masher would cost almost three thousand dollars. There were other things the church—and the missions budget—needed a lot more than a new potato masher.

"We could always have baked potatoes," Ruth Warren said, from the cupboard where she was counting out cups.

Baked? The thought was offensive to Maddy. Baked potato just didn't go with turkey dinner. For one thing, how many children had she seen delightedly making a well in their mounds of mashed potato and easing the gravy in, then making a notch in the wall and watching the gravy flow down the side? Why, it was a way of learning about volcanoes, not to mention having fun at church so they might still want to go when they grew up. And they were supposed to go to baked, where everyone had to struggle with his own potato skin and then some would eat the skins and some wouldn't and gravy would be wasted and there would be much more mess to clean up?

"I suppose we could go to baked," she said.

Ruth closed the cupboard door and moved to one of the silverware drawers. "I don't suppose, in the eternal scheme of things"—before her retirement Ruth taught ancient history two nights a week at the community college—"it matters whether we have baked or mashed. Do you think?" she turned to Maddy, who by now was wiping the masher paddle with a towel.

Maddy wasn't used to thinking in those terms. "I suppose not," she said. But then she thought, *If God cares for the fall of a sparrow, he might care about potatoes.* Somehow holding on to the potato masher made her bold and she said, "Well, if God cares for the fall of a sparrow. . . ." Ruth didn't answer, so she said, "If God numbers the hair of everyone's head. . . ."

Frances Nunnally stood by, checking the dishtowels. "For goodness' sake," Frances said and patted the hairpiece everybody knew she wore, "let's have mashed."

"*If* the masher works," Barbara Allison said. "If Maddy can get it to work." Was there, Maddy wondered, a note of ridicule in Barbara's voice?

· "It'll work," she said. But she wasn't at all sure. She stroked the massive steel bowl as though it were a family pet.

At home that night, Maddy decided—*One more time*. She'd do the potatoes one more time. Then—assuming the potato masher lasted—someone else could do it. She'd show them how. Perhaps she'd go back to working on the fishbowl. She thought of Jeffie, fishing up those earrings. Ten years old. And now he was forty-five and starting to get gray hair.

The trouble began early in the morning of the Turkey Dinner and Bazaar. Maddy hadn't even gotten her breakfast dishes done when the phone rang. It was Ruth Warren. "Maddy, we've just been setting things up for the day, and the masher won't turn."

"Won't turn?" she said, collecting her thoughts. This was to have been her swan song, her last time. Surely the machine wouldn't fail her now. "Are you sure it's plugged in?"

There was an audible sigh. "Of course, it's plugged in." A pause. Then, "Maddy, we haven't started peeling yet. How about we have baked?"

"Oh, let's not have baked." It was unthinkable. "Sometimes it's tricky. Give the plug a little push and see if it doesn't connect."

"All right. Hold on."

She waited. She heard it start—the hum of the potato masher. She'd know that sound if she heard it in a foreign country. But there *was* a catch in it. She doubted if Ruth would detect it.

"It's going!" Ruth exclaimed. "Thanks, Maddy. When will you be down?"

"Oh, about four-thirty. That'll be time enough." If she went too early she'd be tired by the time it came to do the potatoes.

She got there a little after four. They'd start serving at five-thirty. The bazaar was already in full swing. In the ladies' parlor people were milling around among the handcraft items—aprons, embroidered pillowcases with His and Hers in raised letters surrounded by birds done in outline stitches of pink and blue, some stuffed dolls made from patterns at the fabric store, fluffy tulle covers for that extra roll of toilet paper. On another table were the home-canned pickles and jellies, the cookies and loaf breads, then paper napkins with Bible verses in blue letters, bags of nuts ordered from that farm in Georgia. And finally, the fish bowl with Elsa Tomlinson's granddaughter seated behind it, holding the pole with its dangling string and fishhook. Wonderful smells of turkey and dressing permeated the room.

Elsa Tomlinson rushed over to her. "Oh, Maddy, they're looking for you."

She hurried into the kitchen.

"Here she is!" someone said as she came through the swinging door. The carvers were carving, people stood at the stove stirring, two people were chopping giblets. But the biggest crowd had gathered by the end of the counter. She could tell from their faces something was wrong. It must be the potato masher.

Tootie Wilkins turned to her. "It won't go," she said. "We tried to start it for some early take-outs." Tootie looked over at Ruth Warren, who stood tight-lipped on the other side of the machine. "We should have done baked," Ruth said. "We'll never get this thing going."

You should have waited for me, Maddy thought. But she had the good judgment not to say so.

"Are the potatoes cooked?" she asked.

"Of course, they're cooked or we wouldn't be trying to mash some for the take-outs," Frances Nunnally said. "The steam tables are turned on, ready. But this thing"—and she flung her hands wide with impatience at the intransigence of the potato masher. "What are we going to do? We should have more than one person who can work this machine."

Maddy made her announcement. "This is my last time," she said. "I'll write down all there is to know. Or just watch me. Someone else can do it. I'm tired."

For a moment their look was one of alarm, then commiseration, and perhaps a glimmer of understanding why it was so important to her to have this one thing she did better than anyone else. Almost, this time, more than they wanted the potatoes to be ready, they wanted Maddy to triumph over the balky eccentricities of the potato masher.

She walked over to the stove, to the huge kettle mounded with clouds of steam—the first batch of potatoes. She took a long-handled fork and stuck it in. "You're right. They're ready," she said.

"Milk heating?" she asked.

"Right there"—they showed her.

"The butter." She picked up two sticks of butter, stirred them into the hot milk.

She returned to the potato masher, tipped back the motor casing, and inserted the paddle, the little knob fitting into the groove on the housing.

She turned the On knob to the right. Nothing happened.

Ruth Warren said, "Oh, just a minute," and pressed the electric plug deeper into the wall receptacle. The juice connected. The motor began to hum. The women waited; they'd been through this much of it before.

"The problem is the paddle won't turn," Tootie said.

Maddy nodded. There was that funny sticking sound she'd heard over the phone. She remembered it from last year.

"Bring the potatoes," she said.

Ruth and Minna grabbed potholders, lifted the kettle from the stove, and approached the potato masher.

"Pour them in," Maddy said.

They tipped the kettle. The steaming water and jamming potatoes approached the lip, then rumbled into the kettle, splashing drops of scalding water against their aprons. Then the whole rushing stream tumbled in.

"The paddle won't turn, Maddy," Tootie said. "We tried it this afternoon."

"We'll see," she said.

"It's my last time, God," she prayed. "You want these potatoes mashed, turn that motor."

In the kitchen all activity stopped. Carvers, who had had the good judgment to stay away from the potato masher crisis, stood nevertheless with their knives now in midair; stirrers held their spoons hanging like plumblines into the simmering beans, the boiling gravy. Giblet-choppers rested their knives on cutting boards.

Maddy straightened her body beside the huge steel bowl,

pushed the paddle a little tighter into the receiving disc. Then, slowly, she lowered the housing, holding it back so the paddle came down smoothly without a catch or a jerk into the steaming kettle. Again she prayed, "You want mashed? This is our chance. Please."

In from the parlor drifted sounds of the bazaar, and from the dining room where the youth fellowship was setting the tables came the clank of silverware, of salts and peppers going down.

Maddy put one foot on the base of the pedestal of the frame holding the potato masher. She pressed one hand hard against the housing of the motor, leaning the weight of her body against it to push it ever so slightly out of alignment. With the other hand she reached around and, very slowly, a tiny increment at a time, careful not to jerk it, she turned the knob.

At first there was a low buzz, as though the motor were running but the gears wouldn't turn. Then the sound changed. The paddle groaned, began to turn—moving the potatoes and milk like a slow moving puddle. Then, with a whirr, the paddle started to churn. The bowl throbbed. Steam and whirring liquid rose and fell in mounds and vortexes, climbed against the lip of the huge bowl and fell back. Maddy, braced against the mixer, felt energy flow through her seventy-two-year-old body and into that machine and the caroming, careening potatoes becoming a smooth blend of creamy substance, a perfect foil for gravy and turkey and green beans and cranberry sauce.

A cheer went up. The watchers broke into applause, their faces a mixture of astonishment and relief. Then the carvers returned to their carving, the stirrers to their stirring, the choppers to their chopping.

"You're a miracle worker, Maddy," Ruth Warren said and shook her head.

"Not me," Maddy said.

For everything there is a season, and a time for
every matter under heaven:

. . . .

a time to weep, and a time to laugh;
a time to mourn, and a time to dance.

Ecclesiastes 3:1, 4 (RSV)

IT'S ABOUT TIME

alfway between Atlanta and Boston, Gloria put her fork down on the plastic tray of airline lunch—chicken under a mélange of tomato and celery sauce, a dry roll, a square of nameless cake—and said, "I forgot the camera!"

Phil sat back from the forward slant he always assumed for airline meals—his attempt to keep bits of rice, breadcrust, or whatever from landing in his lap. "Well, somebody else will have one," he said.

"But I set it out on the bureau! I never forget the camera, and this is such an important event!"

"Don't worry about it." He picked up a jagged section of roll. "Ed's going to be nervous enough without flashbulbs popping. Especially from his parents. Maybe Katie will have one."

She was disconsolate. "I'd have been careful. How could I forget? Alzheimer's," she muttered and picked up her cup.

Ed had invited them to come up to Boston for the defense of his dissertation. Actually, his wife had suggested it first, knowing what a milestone it would be and how proud they were of him and that he was the last of their children to finish school. Because the job he was moving to was clear across the country in California, he probably wouldn't come back for his formal graduation. So this would be it.

A trip to Boston was always inviting. It was in a way like going home—though it was western Massachusetts where Gloria had grown up and gone to school and to which they had returned many times over the years. Her parents lived in the same house she had grown up in until they died—first her father, then, two years later, her mother.

Her sister lived in the Boston area now and—wonder of wonders—for a while at least so had all three of their sons, though Don and Paula had moved to Michigan last year. But for several years it had been the best geographical bonanza they could imagine—all those loved people in one place. And it was still the densest locus of family. Summer vacations in New England. Thanksgiving at her sister's place in Topsfield. "It's like going home to Mother," she had said, a little teary, the first year after their mother died—this despite the fact that her sister was her junior by almost a dozen years. But age differences mattered less and less as they got older.

After the dissertation defense, there would be champagne and hors d'oeuvres at the lab and, in the evening, a family party at her sister's house. "Can you come?" Ed had asked the question with some misgiving, because, he said, it might make him more nervous to have his parents present.

"Oh, yes," they said—touched and grateful—and made their plans to fly up from Atlanta, where they had moved when Phil took the job teaching philosophy at Emory.

But walking away from the travel agency, tickets in hand, she was swept by a sudden sense of displacement—that they were in the wrong place—that, like the character in *The Man Who Came to Dinner*, they had come here for a while and ended up staying. Was it now fifteen years? And wasn't it time now that they went home? Wherever home was—an odd feeling since the house they had bought when the moved here was more to their liking than any house they had lived in. And furthermore, they had just spent time and money repainting and recarpeting, replacing the last of the frayed vestiges of the previous owner with colors and fabrics of their own choice. "This is going to be it, so we want to do it right," she had told the decorator, who had suggested the slightly discordant tile around the tub could be covered with camouflaging shower curtains. "Nobody will see it. You get into retiling, you're talking big money," he said. "But it's for us," she said. "*We'll* see it. And we won't do this again." Not that she meant to commit herself to this house and city forever, but it was certainly their place, their turf.

And now, suddenly, it felt as though they had best be turning home. Atlanta was all right, but it didn't feel like home—pleasant enough for a while but an improvisation nonetheless.

"It's hard to think of *dying* here," she said to Phil one day, as they were talking about what they might do when he retired a few years hence. It seemed an odd remark to have made. They had talked a number of times about retirement—whether to stay here or go back to New England, where she had grown up, or to Pennsylvania, where he had and where they had lived until the move to Atlanta. "If the children were all in one place—and were going to stay there—it would be tempting to move where they are."

"You know that won't happen," he said.

"I know." Sam would probably stay, being well established now in the financial office of a large medical center. He and Jeri had just bought a home. And had a baby—the first grandchild! But Donald and Paula had already moved, and now Ed and Katie would be moving, too, all the way to California.

"Are you sad about their moving so far?" friends would ask.

"No," she would say. "Boston isn't that close to Atlanta either."

It wasn't the further dispersal of the children that made the boundary remark, "It's hard to think of *dying* here," seem— though a little portentous and self-dramatizing, not to mention borrowing trouble—also appropriate.

Even as she said it, she realized she had crossed some kind of barrier, some stone wall dividing off the fields, to have spoken of dying in any particular place. Of course, they had acknowledged the prospect of dying and had even spoken of the family plot in Massachusetts where their ashes might be buried. But to name a place where this inevitable event might occur was to give it a reality, a particularity, they hadn't done before—images of white sheets and frail shapes beneath them, their own, of relatives present or absent, of medications taken or not taken, their cheeks sunken into their faces, pulled by the gravity of lying flat on their backs, to die.

But why now? she wondered. *What is there about our lives now that I should locate that event tentatively in some place?* They were both well, both had work to do that they liked, in which they had achieved some success and had no intention of leaving, at least for several years.

It wasn't a financial milestone—as though they were suddenly relieved of tuition payments and were therefore prompted to think of new stages of what to do with their money. Ed and Katie had supported themselves—through her work and his fellowships and stipends—since they were married six years ago. So it had nothing to do with any feeling of regret that he was no longer dependent on them—or relief at that, either, to soften the press of whatever it was that seemed so heavy at the prospect of his finishing.

She was out in the garden one day not long before they were to make their trip to Boston when it came to her, pulling weeds from among the iris and the peonies—the blossoms long gone but the foliage still spiny and green—that maybe it was the fact that, with Ed getting his degree at last, they would no longer have a child in school. To be sure, that milestone (the image that occurred to her was that of a turnstile, where you mount a few steps, go through an old swinging gate, and descend an equivalent number of steps into the next pasture) could have occurred in their lives much earlier. Ed, the last of their children to finish, was, after all, thirty-three years old.

Still, to have a child in school seemed a kind of defense—even a denial, perhaps—against being old. *If I have a child in school, I am at most middle-aged, and probably early middle-aged at that.* How many years, after all, had they been going to school open houses and spelling bees and band programs and successive graduations—from junior high, high school, and then college and graduate school? But now the long succession was over. No more being able to say, when asked, "Tell me about the boys," that at least one of them—in this case, the youngest—was still in school.

She gave another yank on the weeds with such force that clods of dirt jumped onto the patio and fragments hit her in the face. Her eyes stung, but not from the dirt. *Oh, God,* she thought. *It's Annie.*

Ed had not always been the youngest. There had been another youngest—a daughter, killed in a mountain-climbing accident on a summer day when they had all been on vacation together. It was a long time ago. Her daughter was sixteen at the time—she would be thirty now—long enough ago for that event not to be, as it had been for years, the single preoccupying fact of her life. But perhaps it loomed on the horizon again in a newly menacing way:

There is no one still in school moved, with scarcely a pause for breath, into *Had Annie lived, she might still be in school*. The fact that Ed had been there somehow filled in the gap of Annie's not being there. It was crazy, she knew it; but somewhere in that groping wish for denial there was a blurred space that, if you didn't look carefully, misted over the fact of Annie's absence because Ed was still there, doing what Annie might have been doing.

It wasn't only school, either, that both announced and also filled in the gap of Annie's absence. (If there were people who did things that Annie might have done—while in some ways this made her absence more conspicuous, at the same time, if you superimposed her image, didn't it make her seem not so far away?)

It was the same as they followed the lives of some of Annie's friends. Some of them had married by now, become mothers. Might Annie have? (This thought was particularly grievous to Gloria, remembering how close she and her mother had been when her own children were born.) A friend of Annie's, with whom she had sung in high school glee club, had gone on to regional opera auditions and had, this past year, made her debut at the New York Civic Light Opera. A cousin of Annie's, younger by ten years, had been accepted at Pratt—which was one of the schools Annie, with her interest in art, was thinking of applying to. Over the figures of each of these young women—as well as those of her two nieces who had been married within the past year—Gloria sometimes superimposed the image of her daughter. As now, she placed her in succession to Ed, who might have been next-to-last to finish. Not last.

The plane was coming down. She looked at her watch. "On time," she said to Phil, who was folding up his papers and putting them back in the carryon.

"Good." He stretched across the space in front of her to look out the window. Circling Logan airport and the bay, she watched the frothing spume of small boats, the hooks of land going into the harbor, the upright columns of skyscrapers like some outlay of toy blocks set onto a game board. "Such a momentous time," she said.

"Who's meeting us?" Phil asked. "Ed and Katie?"

"No, Ed's doing last-minute stuff. Sam is." Dear Sam—at least he and Jeri and the baby would still be in Boston.

At the gate there was Sam with the baby in his arms. "Jeri's at a class," he said after they had all hugged.

"Oh, let me take her." Gloria reached her arms out for the little girl in her lavender sack suit, buried her face against the child's neck, and for the moment forgot everything else—camera, anxiety, the shadowing absence of Annie.

The next morning she and Phil picked up Katie in their rental car. Ed had taken his and Katie's car very early to go to the lab and rehearse his talk one more time.

"Well," Katie said, when they were underway, "how does it feel to have Ed finishing school?"

"Great," Phil said from his place behind the steering wheel.

"I guess so," Gloria said. "How about you?"

"Wonderful! I'm ready for the beaches." Katie, who was from California, had never gotten used to the Boston climate. She leaned forward on the car seat, patted Gloria's shoulder. "Don't look so worried, Mom. Ed'll do fine."

"Oh, I know," she said. "I'm not worried. But it's such a big event."

"The proud mother." Phil patted her knee.

She nodded, the knot in her throat like a stone. "I forgot my camera, Katie," she said.

Katie touched her purse. "I have one. But we'll have to be inconspicuous."

They parked at the edge of the M.I.T. campus and made their way among the towers and pinnacles to the high, modern, science building—white stucco, in view of the Calder sculpture, and the broad gleaming swath of the Charles River. The morning was bright and clear. Gloria reached for Phil's hand as they entered the building. "I'm shaky," she said, "from the excitement."

On the seventh floor they got out, walked down the corridor, past schemes and charts and cartoons from *The Far Side* and *Doonesbury*. Ed was in his office, confident, at ease in his chinos and unironed blue-striped cotton shirt. He hugged them.

"Nervous?" she asked.

"No, I'm ready."

She had been in Ed's office before but not for a while. She was newly impressed—the shelves of books, scientific diagrams and charts, Ed's name in block letters, a few cartoons, a picture of his college softball team. And there—yes—the family, years ago when they were all home, standing in a row by a leaning snow fort. Annie, too. Ed saw her taking in the photo and smiled.

A man came by—pleasant-faced, with dark pants, a rumpled shirt. He touched Ed's shoulder. "You'll do great. Hi, Katie," he said, greeting her.

"Charlie!" Ed turned. "These are my folks. My advisor, Charlie Wellington."

The man shook hands with them each in turn. "Ed doesn't have a thing to worry about," he said. "You can be very proud."

Phil nodded in acknowledgment.

"We are!" Gloria said, trying to keep her smile down to a modest proportion.

She remembered Ed's admonition, "Don't make too much fuss, Mom. O.K.?" How could they not be proud? She would like to have regaled this man with how inquisitive a child Ed had been—always studying, devising experiments. It was no wonder he was covering himself with distinction.

She heard a click. "I just took some pictures," Katie said. They made their way to a modest room with rows of chairs lined up along one wall and shades drawn at the windows—to provide maximum light to the projection screen on which Ed would show his slides. They sat down in the back row behind the assorted students and faculty. "These are all his science cronies," Katie whispered.

The chairman welcomed them all, introduced Ed.

"Thank you all for coming," Ed said. His glance swept along the back row, returned for an instant, moved on. "I'm going to talk about 'Healing of Rock Fractures in Solution,'" he began.

Gloria sat forward, all but holding her breath. She had read some of his scientific papers, had heard him explain with marvelous clarity some of the processes of his experiments. And geology had been for her a wonderful, mind-stretching field of inquiry ever since, as a college freshman needing a physical science to fill out her courses, she had chosen geology almost as a toss-up—"so I don't have to cut up cats." She had found in its images of time, of the motion of the earth's surface, of the life span of rivers, carving their way into valleys, some profoundly moving testament to the creation, to life itself. And here they were, she and Phil, forty years after that first college choice and here was their son, their fine, articulate, knowledgeable, loving child, grown in wisdom and maturity, recognized already as someone who had made original contributions to his field.

The light from the projector beamed across the pointer Ed held in his hand. He touched the screen. "So we don't know just how healing of rock fractures takes place," he said. "There are some puzzles that remain, some surprises." She felt a sudden sting at the back of her eyes. She sat listening to him, understanding some of what he was saying and, for the rest of it, carried along by her pride in him, her rejoicing at his pleasure in the coherences and surprises of the work he was doing, and for the time being, she quite forgot every fragment of anxiety—for him, for themselves, forgot even her nursed and ever-present grief for her lost daughter. Felt, in fact, like standing up and beaming with pride and relief. What had she been fretting about? Look at him!

"Next picture," he said, and another image flashed on the screen. "The flow of water here enhances the healing, the formation of new material."

Because, Gloria thought, *there was no point in life at which everything was settled, everything in place.* Even the earth was always re-forming itself, splitting and healing. So then the trick was not to wait for a perfect resolution but to celebrate the moments of arrival along the way.

And *this* was just such a moment. This was the milestone, sufficient to itself. It was more than sufficient. It was splendid. Totally splendid.

And somehow his arrival at this milestone, as had the arrival of her granddaughter, named Annie by her son and his generous, lovely wife—these gave her permission at last to let fall all cares and cumbrances, as one steps from worn and tired clothes into the freshness of clear water. Permission to let go of the decoy of having a child in school as a defense against aging, let go of the retraction against being almost, undeniably, a senior citizen—which had persisted in seeming a premature designation, not withstanding the drooping chin, the pouches of skin under the eyes that, thank goodness, cleared up by noon.

And Annie, too? To let Annie go?

Yes, perhaps that, too. To relinquish another piece of her grief for Annie, who would be, after all waiting for her, wouldn't she? (She did believe this—a belief she had examined enough during the months after Annie's death that she could almost, now, accept it without having to run through its supportive stories and proofs every time it occurred to her, because she had worn the groove of conviction and faith so deeply back then when she could think of little else.) Whenever she dropped this mantle of her loved—but, yes, deteriorating—flesh and bone and muscle (such as there was) and walked the several steps, ascended to the top of the stile, swung the gate, and stepped into the next field, Annie would be waiting there.

And in the meantime? Ah, in the meantime, there were all kinds of things to do. There was her granddaughter, who also in her being gave a kind of permission to her and Phil to die—even in Atlanta, maybe, though she hoped they would be on a trip to New England, because that was a more fitting place for her to die. But anywhere was fitting, as long as you trusted that it was preliminary, on the way—like stepping onto the stage from the right wing, or the left, or even being dropped on a wire like Mary Martin in *Peter Pan*, or just rising from the audience and stepping over the footlights, through the proscenium arch and onto the stage.

And in the meantime, she would take joy in her work, in her fine young sons, the fine women they had chosen and who had chosen them, in grandchildren as they came along. And when she got home and the papers listed all those courses available at the community college or the high school from which Annie never lived to graduate—why, she might sign up for something. Because even though she didn't need it, it would be nice to have *somebody* in school, wouldn't it?

Two are better than one. . . . For if they fall, one will lift up his fellow; but woe to him who is alone when he falls and has not another to lift him up. Again, if two lie together, they are warm; but how can one be warm alone?

Ecclesiastes 4:9-11 (RSV)

DEAR SALLY . . .

Dear Sally,

Well, here I am in London at the hotel—on my "trip of a lifetime." It was certainly good of you children to urge me to try new things, but I'm not sure this trip was a good idea. I mean, your father and I were going to do this, and even though it's been five years I miss him all over again. Everybody here is in couples. Or at least they're with a friend. On the plane on the way over I met another woman who's alone. She's from Kalamazoo. I told her how we used to sing, "I've got a gal in Kalamazoo," and what a funny name we thought it was. She was not amused. I tried to make it better by telling her how you kids fussed when we thought we might move to Oil City—how we'd defended it, the name of the town. She smiled primly—her displeasure not eased, not one bit.

I tried to sleep on the plane, but then I got hooked on the movie—something like the "Golden Girls"—a bunch of bright silly women on their own. Along comes a man and they fight over him, and the most unlikely one gets him. What a prize! An opportunist gigolo, if you ask me.

I'm tired, of course. I'm glad I paid the extra for a single accommodation. I keep thinking of that woman from Kalamazoo. I think she's a world-class bridge player. Deliver me! What if I'd gotten her for a roommate? When I told her I was from Lansing, she said, "Oh, you're much closer to Detroit than we are," as though Detroit were some kind of contagious disease.

Tomorrow we have a half-day bus tour of the city. I do miss your father so! I'll try to write again soon. Love to Alan. Give little Meggie a kiss from her grandmother. I wish I had her here right now!

Love,
Mother

Dear Sally,

Guess what? It rained all day. I guess that's common for London, but not the best weather for sightseeing. They provided us with big umbrellas, but you had to keep a constant watch or you might get your eye poked by an umbrella spoke. Such a jumble of people! I have to listen really carefully, or I can't understand the people here. And every time you cross the street you take your life in your hands—the traffic all running in the wrong direction. Oh, dear! I wonder if I'm not too old for foreign travel. There are people on this trip who've been to Russia! Can you believe it? One man said, "If you think this is hard to adjust to, think of going to a country where you can't even read the alphabet!" I suppose he's right. If I could have done this when your father was alive, it would have gone much better. I was in a cemetery today and saw seventeen cats! Just think—and no one seemed to be taking care of them. I do miss all of you. Give Meggie a kiss for me.

> Love,
> Your homebody mother

Dear Sally,

Today we visited Westminster Abbey. Of course, I loved it—especially seeing all those heroes (and heroines!) in the Poets' Corner. I still think of my old longing to be a writer. Your father always thought I should try it, but I put it off. And now it's probably too late. That's the trouble—too late for everything.

But the nicest thing happened. There are bookstalls all over this city, and especially all around the Abbey. I was standing there alone, browsing through a pile of books when I heard this voice say, "Oh—*The Princess and the Goblin!*" I looked up and recognized one of the men on our tour. "*The Princess and the Goblin?*" I said. Because, you know, that was one of my all-time favorite books when I was a child. I always felt a little sad that none of you children ever seemed to take to it—no matter how casually I left it around with all those *Little House* books. Anyway, this man—I've seen him with his wife on several of our tours—smiled at me and said, "That book was a mainstay of my childhood."

"Yours, too?" I said, and we had the nicest conversation about the book and how our sense of the world beneath the surface was formed by those tunnels and the little creatures and Curdie and Irene. He told me he hadn't realized until he was a grownup that George MacDonald was known as a theologian too. "Really?" I said. I don't know where I learned that, but I did. It always surprises people—though it seems perfectly natural once you know.

Anyway, we talked a little more, and he asked me if I was enjoying the trip. I said yes, but that traveling alone wasn't as much fun as it would have been if my husband had come. I told him I was sure it was much more pleasant when you had your spouse. (I'd noticed him and his wife—a very distinguished-looking pair—both tall, with curly white hair.) He looked a little odd when I said that about not having your spouse along, but I didn't feel like extending the conversation any more just then. Besides, we had to get back on the bus.

> Much love,
> Mom

Dear Sally,

I picked up my mail at American Express today. Thanks so much for writing. It made me miss you all the more, though. The trip is half over, and I'll be so glad to get home. Tell Meggie to pick out some stories to read together. We're going up to Stratford-upon-Avon this afternoon. I'm so excited about seeing a play there. Some of the other people have opted for more time at Harrod's, but not me.

> Love,
> Your mother

Dear Sally,

We saw *Macbeth*, and it was wonderful. It was done in a rather modern fashion—the three witches were surrealistic figures in some mythic haze. But something else—just before the play started someone said, "Excuse me," and slid past me into the empty seat and sat down. And then said, "Well, hello there," and it was the man I'd had the conversation with about George Mac-Donald. I hadn't noticed him on the bus—I'd sat in front and didn't really notice who else was there. Anyway, he was by himself, and I said, "I guess your wife chose the shopping expedition," and he said, "Oh, that's my sister—and yes, she wanted to pick up some things."

"Oh!" I said, quite startled, of course. "I assumed it was your wife."

"No," he said. "My wife and I parted company years ago."

It was an awkward moment, and I didn't know what to say and so I said, "Oh. Your sister's a handsome woman"—not the brightest comment. And we just sat there. Then he said, "Has your husband been to England often? Or does he not care for travel?" So then it was my turn to correct an impression. "Well, no," I said. "My husband died five years ago. If he had been alive, he would have come." Then I laughed a little bit—I hope he didn't take it as any lack of respect or regard for your father. It's just that the way I'd said it sounded funny to me.

"Oh, I'm sorry," he said. And offered me one of his Lifesavers. I took it, and the play started. I really loved the play.

Tell Meggie her grandmother is having a good time after all.

>   Love,
>   Mother

Dear Sally,

I am getting more adventurous. When we first got here, I was almost afraid to set foot outside the hotel without our guide or some of our party. There have been those terrible stories about the punk rockers in England. And those times when people crush together at sporting events.

But I got a bit more courageous today. I went out onto the street, took a streetcar—I even walked to the upper level, *while the bus was moving*. (I kept my balance and didn't fall.) When I got off downtown, I took a subway—you go down and down into those London subways until you think you must be reaching the center of the earth—and took a train for Kew Gardens. I'd wanted to go, and they put up a sign-up sheet, but I was the only one who signed up so they didn't do a guided tour. I was going to skip it, but then I thought, *Well, I don't know. Maybe I can do it on my own. After all, I have a tongue in my head. I can ask if I'm not sure where I'm going.* I got so used to relying on your father to do those things—to make inquiries. But I don't want to just wither on the vine, as we used to say back in Ohio. (I think they were talking about tomatoes. Or maybe cantaloupe.) Anyway, I had a nice time, got home in time to rest and get ready for the group dinner at some "Ye Olde" restaurant. Your father would have been proud of me. And, maybe more to the point, I was quite proud of myself. I sat with that man I told you about—the one who liked George Mac-Donald—and his sister. His name is George, too. "Maybe that's why I liked George MacDonald," he said. I said, "Maybe that's why I like Emily Dickinson, because my name is Emily."

"Oh, do you?" he said, and we began to tell each other our favorite Emily Dickinson poems. I couldn't remember the next line after "Hope is the thing with feathers," but he remembered it for me. "That perches in the soul," he said. I remembered the last lines, and we said them together. The people sitting by us—including the woman from Kalamazoo—looked quite disapproving, as though we had offended the proprieties. But I felt very light-hearted and didn't even care.

It's unusual to find a man who's that fond of poetry. Your father was—though his taste ran more to Robert Service or Rod McKuen, or that man who wrote about wolves. We used to kid about it. I've thought about him so much on this trip—especially about what it was like when we first knew each other. Tender thoughts, dear. Much love to you and Alan and Meggie.

Mother

Dear Sally,

His sister's name is Victoria. Can you believe it? She's awfully nice. She told me that when they were growing up George used to call her "Queenie" if he got mad at her. Of course, she didn't like it. She says he doesn't do it anymore. "He's really a splendid man," she said, "and a dear brother."

"That's nice," I said. We were standing in the hotel lobby, getting ready for the next trip on the bus—to Windsor Castle. She was a little anxious about his showing up. "George should be here," she said. Just then he came. He had a paper bag in one hand, and he took out two boxes, gift wrapped, and handed one to me! Guess what they were! Bottles of Yardley's English Lavender! I protested, but he said, no, he wanted me to have one to remember the trip.

"Oh, I'll remember it," I said. I was touched by the perfume. Do you remember—I don't suppose you do—how your grandmother often wore Yardley's Lavender? For years I kept a supply. I had other perfumes—some very expensive and much more exotic— that your father had given me. I loved them, too. But I always wore the Yardley's to church—because it reminded me of my mother and how I used to sit beside her when I was little and she would roll little dolls-in-a-swing out of her white linen handkerchief that always smelled of Yardley's. I told George about it. He seemed touched and amused. "Two in a hammock? I don't know that trick," he said. "Sometime you'll have to show me."

I must remember to show Meggie that way of rolling the handkerchief to make two twins lying in a hammock.

> Much love, dear,
> Mother

Dear Sally,

I had a fright last evening, and it made me realize how much has happened on this trip. We were all getting set to leave for a night at the theater to see the Royal Ballet, and George took suddenly ill. He got very pale and dizzy; sweat broke out on his forehead. Terrible, familiar symptoms. Of course, they reminded me of your father's heart attack.

Victoria was there and summoned a doctor right away. It turned out to be nothing serious—perhaps a quick bit of indigestion. But it seemed better that he not go to the theater. I didn't go either. Or Victoria. They assured me he'd be all right—that it was a shame

DEAR SALLY . . .

for me to miss the ballet. "I'd rather stay here with you—if you don't mind," I said, just like that. I suppose it was a bit forward of me. But I said it without thinking. Surprised myself, as well as George.

I wish you could have seen the expression on his face—such a tender gratitude. I was quite moved. "Please stay," he said. "I'm sure I'll recover much faster."

So I did, and after a while we played Hearts, and had a fine visit and told favorite stories about our families and about growing up. And then when we heard the others come in I decided it was time to go to bed, and he walked me back to my room. "It was a much nicer evening than going to the ballet," he said. And then he stayed, and we had the most wonderful conversation for a couple of hours. It was very late when he left, but I wasn't tired. I went to bed and didn't sleep. The line from a poem (I forget whose) kept running through my head—"Not to sleep all the night long for pure joy. . . ."

Now I am feeling sad at the approaching end of this trip. To think that I began with such reluctance! If it weren't for my sense of loyalty to your wonderful father's memory—and to you children . . . I don't know. I have never thought to marry again. I want to be close to you and to watch Meggie grow up knowing her grandmother. But I am having a wonderful time! A few more days, then I'll be coming back.

> Much love,
> Your mother

Dearest Sally,

You may see me before this letter reaches you, but I want to write it, in case. . . . Thank you for the phone call. Of course, you are right. I should have had the courage of my own convictions. Maybe I was a little afraid of what you would think, though I don't know why. I am reeking of Yardley's Lavender. Yes, I *am* a good judge of character, or I never would have married your father. And, of course, nothing is certain. But yes, I do believe the way is always open for new gifts of life. Maybe even for second chances at love. I feel like a school girl. Except school girls don't really know anything about love, about its give and take, its richness and risks.

I will see you soon, dear. And yes, I am bringing a guest. I want you to meet George.

> With a heart full of love,
> Your mother

P.S. Guess what? Victoria and that woman from Kalamazoo—I am feeling much more kindly toward her now—seem to have become good friends!

O Lord, you have always been our home.
Before you created the hills
    or brought the world into being,
    you were eternally God,
    and will be God forever.

Psalm 90:1-2

A Home At Last

They didn't mean to leave the apartment, not for good. But when he fell and it was apparent to both of them that she couldn't take care of him, they allowed the doctor to have him moved from the hospital to Lindenwood. "It'll only be for a little while, dear," he said, his voice husky, because he knew it was another downward step in a long retreat from their dream.

It was a beautiful place—brick colonial exterior, white pillars, a wide porch—"a little like Williamsburg, don't you think?" she had said when they had driven by it soon after it was built. "Yes, it is," he said. He almost always agreed with her on matters of this sort. It was a little odd, this colonial mansion set down in the midst of a macadam parking lot, among mid-city apartments—tenements almost, until they were rehabilitated with federal money and the slow deterioration began again.

There had been an open house for the public, and they had gone after church, still dressed in their Sunday clothes. The sense of bright grandeur suggested by the building's design but made shabby by its setting was fully restored when they got inside. Floral chintz billowed at the windows, covered the groupings of sofas and chairs set on the expanse of jade green carpet, and made a fine backdrop for the mahogany grand piano ("Gift of family of William Green") tucked in one alcove of the large reception/living room. "Oh, it's lovely, isn't it?" she said. "This is the sort of house I'd had in mind for us." Her eyes swept the glass entrance doors, glimpsed again the dulled gray of the parking lot. "You wouldn't even have to look outside if you didn't want to."

The tour included several of the first-floor residents' rooms. Pausing at the succession of the doorways, they nodded benevolently at the white colonial bedspreads, family photos grouped on dressers, an occasional cut-glass carafe and waterglass on a bedside table, or a bouquet of bright flowers.

"It's really quite spacious, isn't it?" she said, and thought ruefully of the piles of unread papers and magazines and boxes that covered virtually every surface of their own residence, the apartment.

"Yes," he said.

"I suppose if you have to come here," and her voice drifted off, "to a place like this, this would be a nice one."

"Yes," he answered, "as long as we're together," and he gave her arm a squeeze. She looked up into his eyes, but he was looking at the thermostat just inside the door. "Look here, Ellie," he said. "Individual controls." He glanced at his watch. "Better hurry if you want refreshments. The open house is over in ten minutes."

They walked down the hall, moving against the flow of visitors coming away from the dining room. At the bulletin board just outside the dining room door she tilted her head to read the week's menus through the bottom of her bifocals.

"Sunday," she read. "Fruit cup, roast sirloin, new potatoes, beans almondine, perfection salad, hot rolls, strawberry mousse." She licked her lips appreciatively. "Mmm, that sounds good."

"Must be a special occasion," he said. "What's perfection salad?"

"I think it's a jelled salad," she said. "Orange and pineapple in an orange gelatin. It's quite good. I used to make it sometimes— maybe for a church supper, or for company."

She said that last softly—moving toward the refreshment table—because the truth of the matter was they hadn't had any company in years. Things were in such disarray at the apartment—hardly any room for extra people to sit, let alone to clear the big oak table for a stately meal. She and Mel ate in the kitchen. "When we get things sorted out," she often said, "we'll have people in."

They didn't neglect their host and hostess duties. They invited people out to restaruants, where they could all sit comfortably and visit and no one had to be hopping up and down, getting things and clearing the table. And where she didn't have to be embarrassed by the papers and books or explain to her sister-in-law, Doris— who had a much bigger place, a whole house, and, of course, was able to keep it neater—why it was taking them so long to sort through things, catch up with the papers and magazines, decide what to do with the extra furniture that had come down through the family.

"I'd be glad to help you, Ellie," Doris said, with that avid look that told her Doris could hardly wait to see to what new degree of disorder the apartment had fallen.

In the early years of her marriage to Mel they had thought of the apartment as only a temporary dwelling. "Until we get a house," she would say, looking at him expectantly—her love always paramount—deferring to his judgment, his wisdom.

"That's right," he had said, as though he believed it, too.

From time to time, back then, they'd gone to various Sunday afternoon open houses of property for sale. She was so appreciative, so lingering in her examination of each room, so lavish in her praise that they were always accorded careful attention by the real-estate person. "We're not quite ready to make a decision," she would say, receiving the salesperson's card and smiling tentatively. "We'll let you know," and they would go home to talk about the merits of each house.

There was, of course, always some critical flaw. "The living room is quite small for entertaining," she would suggest. "Yes, you're right about that," he'd say. Or she'd say, "I'd really like a bath for each of the guestrooms." "Sure," he'd say, and with a mixture of relief and regret they would, again, acknowledge that the apartment was home for now. But always it would in their minds give way to some splendid house, where her lovely old family pictures and bric-a-brac—the Rogers Group, the Boehm birds, the Limoges plates—could be displayed in a more appropriate setting.

Theirs had been an uneven match. She was a college graduate, and he hadn't finished high school. "He had a vision problem—he couldn't see the blackboard," she would say, if the subject of his limited education ever came up. He was a good man, had a good clerical job in the accounting department of a local mill. He made an adequate salary. He read a lot, and he never made a grammatical error. He was five years her junior. He had courted her for nine years, until, close to forty, her expectations had eroded and he was, at last, a suitable mate.

They were married in the living room of the house she had shared with her widowed mother. Her brother's two young daughters attended her in watered blue silk dresses with velvet sashes, along with her best college friend—a spinster teacher from Wisconsin—in a rose taffeta evening gown. Her mother wore a floor-length gray lace gown. She was resplendent in ivory satin, with a lace tiara and flowing marquisette veil. Her brother, Walter, gave her away. Her father had been dead for twenty years.

For their honeymoon she and Mel went to a hotel in a nearby town, and during the daytime drove around looking at lovely old New England houses and antique shops, stopping to eat at country inns where she would examine the decor with an eye to the house they would have someday.

Mel had a nice apartment in one of the newer developments off the park, and she moved in with him—"until we get established," she explained to Doris and Walter. There was no possibility of children. (She had had to have a hysterectomy in her mid-thirties.) Doris, mother of three, confided to a friend that it was a good thing—"Ellie could never keep up with a baby."

They rented a truck and, with the help of some of Mel's co-workers, moved some of the fine Victorian furniture from the house Ellie had lived in into the apartment. Mel had some nice old pieces from his family, too. With the addition the apartment was crowded, but they kept it all against the day they would buy a house. "If we ever do," Mel said, already not quite believing.

He had already shed some dreams. He had a fine tenor voice; and for a while, under the enthusiasm of a high school choral director (he had attended high school for two years), had been encouraged to think about a singing career. When he left school, he had nowhere to sing until, in his mid-twenties, he joined a church choir—which was where he met Ellie. He was soon chosen to sing solos. "He really should have gone on the concert stage," Ellie would say. He would look abashed and grateful. She, who had been to college, had even studied music education, would listen deferentially while he spoke of opera and symphony and chorale.

The move from concert career to church choirs had been analagous in some ways to many of the dreams they'd had—at first, singly and then, after their long-delayed marriage, together.

Ellie did everything she could to bolster Mel's self-esteem, from explaining his curtailment of education because of "the vision problem" (his family hadn't been able to afford glasses), to writing in "financier" on her college questionnaire asking the nature of spouse's employment.

Instead of a financier—he did have an aptitude for figures—he became treasurer of the Sunday school, and after church each Sunday you could find him at his desk piling nickles and quarters into stacks to encase in paper rollers and, eventually, take to the bank.

Twice a year they would attend the opera productions that came on tour, and about once a year they would take the train to Boston or New York and stay in a hotel and go to a play—experiences which would suffuse her for weeks thereafter with a glow of accomplishment, as though succeeding in the effort to see these things was tantamount to filling one's life, beginning with one's home, with a kind of splendor. So that they lingered a little longer over after-dinner coffee when they took Walter and Doris to the local hotel for dinner and felt justified, at last, in claiming equal time to tell of their exploits, equal to Doris's ever-ready account of her children's prowess in school or, later, success in careers and marriages.

When Walter and Ellie's mother died, they had, of course, to clear the house. Walter didn't want much—Doris didn't either, having absorbed a household of antiques from her own parents, who had died a number of years before. "Let's give it away— maybe to the Old Folks' Home?" Walter suggested. "The things that aren't especially valuable could go to Goodwill."

But Ellie would not hear of it. "Your daughters may want some of these things some day," she remonstrated. "Some of the finer pieces we could use in the apartment. Or"—she hesitated because already, even for her, the dream had lost much of its urgency—"we could use them if we get a house."

"What about Mother's house?" Walter asked—because there it was.

She sighed. "It's pretty small," she said, "and it would need a lot to bring it up to date."

She put some of the furniture in the storage room in the apartment basement. But into their bedroom already crowded with a double bed, two nightstands, a chifforobe, a highboy, and a horsehair-upholstered rocker with a petit point footstool, she put a desk and another highboy, making it possible to reach the bed—set against the middle of the long wall—from one side only. "Your side, dear," Mel said. "I don't mind passing you on my way into bed. Who knows what might happen?"—his laughter suggesting their passionate encounters might interrupt his passage along the hand-carved walnut footboard. Her mother's jewelry and other small effects she stored in boxes under the bed, in the kneehole of the desk, or high in the all-but-unreachable cupboard already crowded with scarcely opened wedding gifts—sets of crystal and china, a banquet cloth of heavy Irish linen with twelve matching napkins, ornate tureens, tier plates for setting out petits fours or fancy sandwiches at the afternoon tea parties she had anticipated when these gifts were received.

The ultimate disposition of these valuables hung heavy on her mind. As the years went by, she would sometimes take a few pieces from a box or chest and, holding them to the light, try to picture them in the possession of one of her nieces—Doris and Walter's two daughters and Mel's four nieces by his two sisters, who lived downtown in adjoining houses near the bus station.

Sometimes, when she knew she would be with one of the nieces, she would take with her a gold chain with a garnet drop or a locket still containing tiny childhood pictures of herself and Walter and, drawing her niece aside, would hold the necklace against the child's throat, and ask gently, "Do you like this, dear? I'm trying to decide who should have it." Or she would produce a small pho-

tograph of an obscure ancestor, framed in a lovely antique frame—
"Now, do you remember who this is?" She would wait, archly
watching, always hoping they would know. Usually they didn't.
They always pretended interest in the photographs, because, for
all her peculiarities, they loved Ellie, found her an oasis of extended calm in an often frenzied world, and because they did in-
deed like the garnet necklace and the gold locket and would be
happy to have them some day.

As she and Mel got older, the debris in the apartment grew more
dense—unread magazines, sections of the Sunday paper saved for
later perusal, letters from friends, which were eventually answered
but never thrown away. By now the dream of a house had dropped
away. Now her hope was to somehow organize her possessions,
take command, make some order of the piles of paper, scrapbooks,
old photos that increasingly narrowed the aisles, diminished the
living space. Maybe then she might be willing to part with some of
the furniture, now that her nieces were starting to establish homes
of their own.

Then one day, going down to the storage unit searching for some
item Ellie had suddenly missed and felt she needed, Mel, whose
"vision problem" had long since been corrected with glasses but
was now returning with beginning cataracts, fell on the steps and
broke his leg. It was not a serious fracture, but it undid the deli-
cate balance by which the two of them had been able to function as
one unit in the world. So, at the end of his hospitalization, he went
to Lindenwood; and she went with him. They had money enough.
It had never really been lack of funds that kept them from realizing
their dream of a more gracious life, but lack of energy and will to
confront the many choices and take the many initiatives necessary
in a major life change.

"Of course, we'll go back to the apartment," they told Doris and
Walter when they came to visit them in Lindenwood. "But this is
fine for now," Ellie said, stretching her legs into the empty space
in front of her chair. "We want to be sure Mel is able to get around
well before we go back," and she smiled lovingly at him, propped
up in the bed, the ribbed cotton spread neatly folded across his lap.

It was their neighbors in the apartment who told them of the burglary. Coming home one afternoon, Mrs. Simpson next door had seen the door wide open and had called the police. After investigating, an officer came to Ellie and suggested that she come with him to give him an inventory of what had been stolen.

Shocked, grieved, she kissed Mel lovingly and went back with the kind officer to the apartment. It was a shambles—papers strewn everywhere, drawers opened and dumped out. "If you'll tell us what's missing?" the officer said tentatively, looking over the chaos.

She went right away to the silver chest. Empty. The box of her mother's jewelry that had been under the kneehole desk—gone. "Oh, oh," she sat on the very edge of the bed, lost in unconsolable sorrow.

The officer tried to comfort her. "If you'll give me a list, ma'am, it's possible we'll find some of it."

"I don't know. I don't know." She began to search around for paper, pencil. "I can't seem to find any paper to write on," she said.

"Here, ma'am." The officer produced a pad and pencil.

She took it. "Let's see. There was an opal ring—four little stones—well, not so little either, exactly the same size," she told him. "My grandfather had been given them by a wealthy acquaintance he had befriended. The acquaintance owned a jewelry store, and this was one of his finer pieces. I had it appraised—it had a lovely gold filigree setting. I had to have one of the prongs tightened. The jeweler here told me the opals were very fine quality."

"Yes, ma'am," he said.

"And the silver was our wedding silver—twelve place settings. We were given everything but fish forks and iced teas and we added them, a piece at a time, over the years." She saw him eyeing the sink where pocked and tarnished tableware, the plate worn through to copper, sat in the drainer. "We used other things, serviceable, for everyday."

"Yes, ma'am." He looked at his watch. "Suppose I take you back to—your place—and you can do the list there?"

"Oh, I guess so," she said and gathered up her purse and giving a grieved look at the confusion all around, she followed him to the car, and they returned to Lindenwood. "If I were you, ma'am, I'd clear that place out," the officer said as he opened the door for her to get out. "A place like that—no one living there—it's a sure invitation to burglars."

"Do you think so?" she said. "Oh, I hope not."

They called the landlord, who had the locks changed. But burglars came a second time, and then a third. "You'd think there was something they could do to stop them!" she said, irate, to Walter and Doris.

"We'd have been glad to help clear it out for you," Doris said.

"Thank you," she said and shook her head sadly. "You wouldn't have known what to do with the things."

So they kept the apartment, and when Mel got better and was able to drive, they went over every month or so and tried to straighten things out, see if they could find any clues (the police had been unsuccessful in their search for suspects—or stolen goods, since a list had never been forthcoming), muse fondly about the remaining treasures, commiserate about the whirlwind confusion of everything, and then, relieved, go back to their sun-filled room, the spaciousness of the living rooms and halls, the sociability with the other residents, the reliable comfort of pleasant meals provided by someone else.

Until one day she realized they had moved. The apartment was still there, and probably would be, in their names until they died. But their home was here, with the grand piano against the flowing glazed chintz drapery, among the stately halls down which they walked to the gracious dining room.

"I feel years younger," she said one day soon after this realization came to her. They were readying themselves for dinner. "We'd have to leave it anyway, eventually." She felt suddenly light-headed. "After all these years," she said, "I think I've just stopped caring about a lot of it." And she looked at him in wonderment.

"It was too much," he said. "It was always too much."

When he heard the bell sound in the hallway, he offered her his arm. "My lady," he said, and she took it and they walked arm in arm down the broad carpeted hallway, under the glass chandelier of the jade-carpeted living room, and into the dining room, where, as sometimes happened—for the monthly birthday celebration or the meetings of the board of directors—the room glowed with the light of a hundred candles.

"Oh, look, it's a special occasion," she said, and she offered her arm in turn to old Mrs. Webster, who stood hesitant and alone. "Come and eat with us, why don't you?"

"Why, thank you," the old woman said. Together the three of them found places at the table. Sitting in the glowing light, Ellie looked around at the rows of faces she had perhaps hardly seen. Observing how the candlelight played on aging features, she thought of people she had loved, somehow made more vivid to her in this new sense of home. Why, a couple of tables away, a woman in a rose-colored dress and with light glinting off her glasses, could almost have been her mother. And there, beyond Mel, facing away from them but his profile clear against the soft fall of drapery framing the window—its darkened glass reflecting back the light of the candles—was a man who looked for all the world like her favorite Uncle Harry, on whose farm she had spent some enchanted childhood summers, and who had died years ago in a trawling accident on Casco Bay.

"You never know, do you?" she said to Mrs. Webster, who, in the buzz of conversation, the sounds of water being poured and utensils scraping against bowls, didn't hear, but nodded and smiled back anyway—as though whatever Ellie had said was just fine with her and wasn't it a lovely evening?

When they met, Joseph threw his arms around his father's neck and cried for a long time. Jacob said to Joseph, "I am ready to die, now that I have seen you and know that you are still alive."

Genesis 46:29-30

OH, THAT I KNEW WHERE
I MIGHT FIND HER

n a reservation in northern Wisconsin, a wizened, frail woman had all but abandoned hope of ever seeing again in her lifetime her dead daughter's child.

Sometimes, in the first dew of evening, Minnie Newsome would leave the modest frame house she shared with her son, Bucky, and her two grandsons, Sam and Grit. Walking to the grove of trees at the edge of the reservation, she would sit on a half-rotted log and, cradling her arms and swaying back and forth in a maternal rhythm as old as the pounding of the blood, would try to find, in the hidden recesses of her imagination, some trace of the child. Was she alive? Where was she? Of course, she would not be a baby now, this child they had parted with when she was barely a week old—a tiny creature, red-faced, with a shock of black hair, eyelids still swollen from birth, arms flailing in the random, jerky movements of the newborn. Minnie kept careful track of the child's age—eighteen next August. But it was always as a baby that she saw her. A baby lost. Never to be seen again except in those yearnings of the imagination.

Until the call came.

She could still see Bucky lumbering from the house—his tan flannel shirt hanging over his faded jeans, flapping around his big body—coming toward her in the grove where she stood watering her yellow daises. Something about his gait alerted her before she saw the look on his face—a kind of arrested stare, as though he would not commit himself in any way to what he had heard. "Ma, there's a call for you." He paused. "Somebody looking for Rosalie."

"Rosalie!" Her daughter had been dead for five years. "Who is it? What did you tell them?"

"Nothing. I thought you'd better tell them."

She went inside. "Hello?"

"Mrs. Newsome?"

"Yes."

"This is Brenda Arnold, in Chicago. I'm a social worker with an organization called Parent Finders. We're trying to learn the whereabouts of your daughter, Rosalie. I wonder if you can help us?"

"Rosalie's dead," she said. "Who wants to know?"

"Her daughter."

For an instant Minnie was stunned, her throat all but closing. She sat down on the sofa and with her free hand clamped onto the hard edge of the wooden frame. "Where is she?"

"In Pennsylvania. She's fine. She'd like to learn more about her family of origin, perhaps even meet them." The woman hesitated. "Her father?" she asked.

"Humpf! Try and find him. Maybe he's somewhere in Chicago. I'm her grandmother. I'm her family. I've been waiting."

They talked some more. The girl's name was Rachel. She'd been adopted right away by a Chicago family who had since moved to Pennsylvania. They could drive her out here as early as next week—"if that's acceptable," Brenda Arnold said.

"Have her come. There's lots of family here," she said. Her mind leaped along the row of cousins, aunts, and uncles who lived close by. She saw their faces—blank, astonished, then breaking into smiles of welcome.

"I'll talk to them. I'll call you," Brenda Arnold said.

She told Bucky, who shook his head in disbelief and went off to tell the others. Then she went to sit in her grove of trees and rock back and forth, her heart a churning jumble of elation and dread. What would it be like? Who was this girl, stepping out of years of silence and absence, a girl missed, longed-for but never expected? What would she look like? What would they say to one another? What would she tell her about the mother who had died five years ago, lines of bitterness and dissolution carved into her face so she looked like an old woman when she wasn't even thirty?

Rosalie was sixteen when the infant girl was born. Not married. Still attending the crude school at the edge of the reservation, still trying to master the elements of English grammar—diagraming sentences taken from the works of British novelists and play-wrights. She was beautiful—tall, the flush of apples on her full cheeks, the glimmer of burning ashes in her large dark eyes.

The baby's father was a schoolmate. They were children themselves—Rosalie the baby of the family, youngest of four, born when Minnie was forty-two and thought her days of childbearing were over. "My baby," she would croon, leaning over her with the wonder of a first-time mother—such a gift this child had seemed. "Sweetening our age," she had said to Joe, who had seemed, as she had, to be made young again by the advent of the baby.

Rosalie's childhood had been easy, though the small house was crowded for a family of six—two of them always had to sleep in the hide-a-bed in the living room. Rosalie was the family pet. The older children doted on her, helped care for her, dressed her in her prettiest clothes, spent part of their meager earnings to buy her candy and toys from the reservation store, until their parents protested, "You'll spoil her. Besides, we need the money for food."

Then, one by one the others moved out of the house to establish their own homes and families. Rosalie at last had a room of her own. She worked hard in school. She won an essay contest in eighth grade on "My Ambition." She wanted to be a teacher, live in a big city like Milwaukee. There was a mission school in Kansas. Maybe she could go there after high school.

But when she got to high school she began to turn from her dream of college. By now she wanted to be a movie actress. "But how can I ever get to Hollywood? And even if I did. . . ." She eyed the photos in the movie magazines—stalk-thin women with blond hair and slender faces. "Besides, none of my friends are going to college."

It was about that time that Bucky and his wife divorced. "Irreconcilable differences," the decree read. "I married too young," Jane Anne insisted. "I never knew who I was." She took off for the city, and after a while Bucky, who said he was going crazy out there on the edge of the reservation without her, brought his two sons and moved back home. So once again the house was crowded.

Rosalie spent more and more time away from home. She had a girlfriend with whom she sometimes stayed when it wasn't a school night.

"She could come here," Minnie offered.

"Where? What could we do here?" Rosalie demanded, looking around the living room crowded with the hide-a-bed, TV, two chests of drawers, a table and chairs.

"Well, what do you do there?" Joe asked.

"We watch TV. We have parties, invite friends over."

Sometimes a young man from the reservation school came by and picked Rosalie up in a beat-up car. He was sixteen. They had no idea Rosalie was sleeping with him.

They learned she was pregnant when one morning, getting ready for school, she came, ashen-faced, to Minnie, "I think I'm going to have a baby!" She barely made it to the bathroom before she threw up.

She had dropped out of school as soon as she began to show. It was school policy—no pregnant girls. At the reservation office they were told of an agency in Madison that would take the baby for adoption.

"Are you sure we can't keep it?" Minnie and Joe asked each other the agonizing question again. They were almost sixty years old and not in good health. Their other children had all they could do to feed and clothe their own families. "We must think of the child, the child's future," Minnie said. Sullen, withdrawn, frightened, Rosalie agreed.

They had given the baby to the social worker from the agency when she was eight days old and her tiny red face was just beginning to lose the swellings of her travail in entering the world. Rosalie had given her a name—Linda. Minnie saw the social worker write down on the form "Baby: F."

"Her name is Linda," she said.

The woman shook her head. "Her adoptive parents will give her a name of their choice," she said. They signed the papers and drove away in the car.

And that was the end of it. Except, of course, that it wasn't.

At first Rosalie seemed relieved to have the pregnancy over. At eighteen and graduated from high school, she married and settled into a small house not far from her parents. Though she wanted children she never got pregnant again. When in desperation she went to a doctor in Ashland, he told her she had had an infection that would make it impossible for her ever to conceive. She got drunk first and then came and hurled the accusation at her parents—"I had a beautiful baby, and you made me give her away!"

Minnie flinched and said nothing. Lying awake at night, staring into darkness, she went over and over it. Had they done the right thing? "If we had known this would be her only child . . . ," she said softly, unsure whether Joe was asleep or awake.

He stroked her cheek. "We didn't know," he said. "How could we know? Besides, we had to think of the baby."

"The baby," she said.

Over the next years Rosalie turned increasingly to alcohol. Her recriminations against her parents were never absent for long from the dark eyes, the rapidly aging face. Every time the baby's birthday came around, she got drunk. Shortly before her twenty-ninth birthday, she died of liver failure, her face the haggard, lined face of an old woman.

"Well, she's gone," Joe said as they walked away from the cemetery. "She's done blaming us for everything."

"Not everything," Minnie said, her heart twisted, unwilling to acknowledge the extent of the breach that had grown between her and her youngest child. It wasn't all Rosalie's doing, either. She had been angry herself, and had told Rosalie so—hadn't she and Joe done the best they could—more for Rosalie than for any of the others, even setting aside a little money so she could go to college? And this was the payment parents got—accusations and sullen looks? And now—the ultimate abandonment—Rosalie had died and left them.

Joe's health was failing too. An old logging accident had caused the deterioration of a hip joint so that he moved with difficulty and was in frequent pain. One day the year after Rosalie died he went out to help friends fell a tree. They brought his body home on the truck—"a freak accident," the men said, something about the saw slipping, the log falling the wrong way. She buried him in a grave next to Rosalie.

So now it was she and Bucky and his two grown children living in the house. She was past seventy when Joe died. Over the years she had developed angina. Often now she had to sleep sitting up in a chair in the living room and even the nitroglycerin couldn't control the sometimes wild beating of her heart.

"I won't mind dying," she said to Bucky one evening when they sat on the porch watching the fireflies flit in the dark night. "Of course, there are some things I regret, things I wish had turned out different." She paused. "Thank God, your children have more chances now than you kids did."

It was true. One of Bucky's boys had gone to study ethnology in Oklahoma and come home with his hair in two long braids over his shoulders. Another grandchild was well on his way to being manager of one of the reservation stores, and a granddaughter was studying dentistry in Milwaukee.

"You've done a lot for us, Ma," Bucky said. "You better stick around now and enjoy it." He put a hand out and patted her arm, and she knew he was trying to comfort her for the losses she'd borne—Rosalie dying, and then Joe.

"I wish we had a picture of Rosalie," she said. "I mean before she got to looking so old and sick."

She remembered Rosalie as a baby. She had looked remarkably like that infant they had handed over to the social worker from Chicago. The same fat cheeks and dark hair. But the image of the girl at fifteen or sixteen, beautiful, strong, seemed lost to her memory. The Rosalie that haunted her mind was a woman old before her time, her body wasted, her eyes burning with that reproachful look she turned on Minnie so frequently—as though it was Minnie's fault she had gotten herself pregnant at fifteen, Minnie's fault she had given up the only child she would ever bear, Minnie's fault she had succumbed to the disease of alcoholism and looked so haggard and old.

And what of Rosalie's daughter? Minnie, who sometimes had difficulty recalling her own age, could have told at any time the exact age of "Baby: F." And when the girl would have been of an age to travel on her own, she scrutinized every visitor to the reservation, hoping against all reason that somehow the girl, growing up, would have known where she belonged and return to her own—like the birds who, taken from their nest in infancy and raised in an alien setting, will, when they go to build their own nest, build the nest of their own kind—twig for twig, location for location, sealer for sealer. Or might that girl, too, have died? It was, after all, getting on toward twenty years. But in her occasional crooning, swaying interludes on the decaying tree, she did not think so. The girl was alive. But where was she?

It was when she was about fifteen that Rachel Oglethorpe, the black-haired, black-eyed daughter in a family of blonde, blue-eyed parents and children, began to burn with a secret hunger to know who her real parents were. Ever since she could remember she had known she was adopted. "With the others, we took what we got. But we chose you," her adoptive parents would remind her on the occasions—increasingly frequent as she got into her teens—when she would bridle against the unfixable fact that everyone else in the family looked the same. Only she looked different.

Her adoptive family, enlightened and loving people, bought her books on American Indian culture, bought prints of American Indian scenes for her room, and once, when a traveling craft fair in a distant town featured American Indian crafts, they took a picnic and made a day-long perusal of the fair. She was astonished at the beauty of blankets and pots but more astonished—and with a feeling of ineffable homesickness—to see so many people who looked like her. Going through school, she knew her appearance was a startling change from the four blond brothers and sisters who had preceded her. Teachers never spoke of it; surely it was on her record that she was adopted and they would have been too polite to mention it. But sometimes a schoolmate would express incredulity—"You sure look different"—or she could just tell from their puzzled expressions that they were trying to figure it out. Then she would say, "I was adopted," and it would be fine.

Except as she grew older, it wasn't fine. What had happened? Who was she really? Sometimes she would cry herself to sleep at night, wondering about the mother who had abandoned her—how could she give away a child! Her sadness turned to anger. She began to skip school, to chafe at her share of household chores.

Once, when she had just acquired her driver's permit, she took the car without permission, drove around town alone for an hour and, coming home in a panic that she might be discovered, smashed into a tree.

Her parents, frightened, took her to a counselor. "Maybe," he said, after talking with the family and finding no major errors of judgment to explain her behavior—"Maybe"—he rubbed his hand through his thinning brown hair and looked at Rachel—"Maybe you need to find your birth parents. Is that possible?"

Startled, she turned to her mother, her eyes wide now with a new hope. "Is it?" she asked.

"We'll contact the agency where we got you," her mother said. "We'll see what they can do."

Well, they should be coming soon, Minnie thought, standing in front of the bathroom mirror, trying to settle her hair. Coming to see her and Bucky and Steve and Grit and the other relatives who would be rushing over as soon as they saw a Pennsylvania car drive up. They had planned stories to tell, family mementoes to share with her. What would her granddaughter look like? Like Rosalie? All she could see of Rosalie was that haggard face, the reproachful eyes.

Her heart raced. She drew a glass of water and took another pill. This was not the calmness her doctor recommended. But she didn't care. Didn't care a twitch of a dog's tail or a fragment of tree bark or the ascending smoke from any ceremonial fire. Because once she saw the child, she would be satisfied. She looked at her scarred Timex again and went out onto the porch. Any minute now.

When she saw the trail of dust coming from the highway, she stood up. She could see the car now—a blue car, not large. It stopped and the back door swung open, and out stepped a tall, long-legged, young woman. Minnie sucked in her breath. It was an apparition! High cheekbones, hair soft around her shoulders. As she came closer, Minnie saw the flush of apples on her full cheeks, the glimmer of burning ashes in her large, dark eyes. The girl approached her, and they looked at one another for a single minute, checking with the infallible wisdom of the heart to be sure, to be sure who they were to one another. The girl stretched out her arms. "Grandmother!" she said.

"Rosalie," Minnie whispered.

Then she stepped to the edge of the porch. For a minute she held the girl at arms' length. "Why!" she said, while the picture formed before her eyes and proclaimed its long-hidden form and feature and she felt some deep forgiveness leaping from her heart and the heart of a daughter long gone who could be standing before her now, this minute, and who surely must be watching from somewhere in the air around them. "Why, Rachel!" she exclaimed. "You're the spit 'n' image of your mother!"

Do not be anxious about tomorrow, for tomorrow
will be anxious for itself. Let the day's own
trouble be sufficient for the day.

Matthew 6:34 (RSV)

A WELL-ORDERED LIFE

For the first few months after her retirement as head of the English department at Public School 204, Rebecca Lindaman had plenty to do. For one thing, it was wonderful to lie in bed a few extra minutes, looking at the striped wallpaper—blue and green, with small abstract patterns of blue and green flowers between the stripes. She noted again how the stripes exactly framed her mother's antique mahogany mirror, the edges of the frame just touching the broadest blue stripe on either side. It pleased her, as it pleased her how well the antique walnut chest and small walnut end table fit on either side of her bed, outriggers against the world, securing her in place. During the years of her teaching, she had often piled school papers on the chest and read a few before she turned off the silk-shaded glass light and went to sleep.

And it was wonderful to have lunch at home. At school, if you didn't have lunchroom duty, you ate in the teachers' lunchroom, but it was always noisy and until recently, when by court order they had set aside a separate room for teachers who smoked, it was apt to be full of cigarette smoke as well. Now she fixed herself a nice lunch, put it on the hammered aluminum tray, and took it in to the den, where she ate it slowly while watching the midday news.

The news lasted half an hour and was done by a local anchorman and weather forecaster; and when occasionally she would pass these people on the street or at some fund-raising event, she would nod benevolently. The news was punctuated by several commercials, and she developed some fondness for the man who extolled the virtues of a reclining chair for people who couldn't raise themselves to a sitting position. His smoothly caring words were followed by film clips of aged movie stars demonstrating the chairs. She was relieved to be fully supple still herself—a condition she maintained by swimming regularly at the local Y, as she had done when she was still teaching.

Immediately after the news a soap opera came on with no intervening announcement or commercial. She had scorned soap operas as maudlin and a waste of time, and she always shut off the TV as soon as the first commercial arrived, but to her own bemusement she found herself, for a few minutes at least, an interested voyeur to the lives of Ridge—or was it Rich?—and the several blond, blue-eyed young women with whom he seemed to be involved. This noontime interlude of television along with her lunch was in a way foolish—she would see all the news in the evening anyway. It was an indulgence she allowed herself, though with some misgiving, especially in regard to those moments she spent watching "The Bold and the Beautiful."

The first summer after her retirement was much like all the other summers, except there was no question about taking teaching-enrichment courses. She usually spent a week at the ocean with her brother and sister and their families—whoever could come, which usually meant, in addition to her, at least Sam and Bethanne and Janet and Ridley and several of her nieces and nephews and at least one or two babies in the next generation. It was a wonderful time; she looked forward to it all year. They rented several cottages at a place near Nag's Head. She would stay with one family or another, whoever happened to have a spare bedroom that year. The other family members at least pretended to consider her a prize. "Please, can we have Aunt Rebecca this year?" one of the nieces had said this past year when, after a family wedding in the spring, they were planning their next summer's reunion.

Some summers she spent a week with her girlhood friend in Bucks County who, like her, had never married. The rest of the summer she worked in her garden, read, went to a movie or a concert with a friend, and went to church and to the monthly meeting of the church women.

One summer when retirement was still ten years away, she had gone on a cruise to Scandinavia, fulfilling a lifelong dream to sail among the fjords—those craggy towering white cliffs that had so enchanted her in the fifth-grade geography book. On the last morning of the cruise, as she sat in the dining room watching through the huge picture window while the ship—its red and white flag flapping in the bright sun—moved through the narrow V-shaped gorge of Hardangerfjorden, she took another sip of coffee and a bite of apricot-filled pastry and thought, *When I retire, I'll travel a lot*. But as the time for retirement actually drew close, she put off making plans for any extensive travel until she could, as she put it, "get settled."

"Settled?" her sister Janet had said. "I should think you'd want to get *un*settled, do new things."

"Well, yes," she said, "but I'll have to plan it out, see what I'm able to manage."

It wasn't as though she wasn't prepared for retirement. She'd taken courses on it—the importance of financial planning and having what was generically known as "other interests." She nodded, wrote down a few notes on these sensible steps of what one was supposed to do. She had always planned for her future; this was nothing new to her.

There were, in fact, few things in her life—for which preparation was possible—that she hadn't been prepared for. She had planned her finances carefully over the years, so, what with her school pension and social security and a modest inheritance from her parents which she had put in a conservative mutual fund and the prospect of being able to receive Medicare, she felt she was protected against financial disaster. She owned her small home, her car was paid for, and she didn't need to use it daily since she lived in walking distance of shops and church. She tried to walk places when she could. It was good for her. The same with food, she ate very sensibly—eggs no more than once a week, fish, vegetarian pastas, dishes with beans and rice, dessert hardly ever other than fruit (and that usually apples or bananas—sturdy, reliable fruits). No worry about importing exotic diseases from faraway islands. Two cups of coffee a day, and that half decaf.

But now this golden opportunity of retirement—and what was she to do?

At the family reunion that first summer, the others had all kinds of suggestions. Travel, of course. They pored over the Elderhostel catalog together.

"Look here!"

"They even go to Hawaii!"

"You could start with one near home. Philadelphia? The Liberty Bell?" her great-niece suggested.

"I'll see."

Yes, the courses and locations looked interesting, not too expensive. Many were held on college campuses with dormitory accommodations. She wasn't sure she wanted to have to walk down the hall at night to go to the bathroom.

Her nephew, who had a beginning job as a computer operator in a big New York law firm, invited her to visit. "Stay with me," he said. "We'll do the town." She had stopped by once at the apartment he shared with two other young men. They told tales of roaches who scuttled in huge and daunting freedom into—and out of—the "Roach Motels" they placed around the apartment. Their guest arrangement was a mattress which leaned against the living room wall—a backrest for seated visitors—to be taken down and laid on the floor for sleeping. She thanked him.

Her niece with the two-year-old twins urged her to come for an extended visit. "Thank you," she said. She loved the twins, but right now a week of them was enough.

She got through the summer all right. She spent her week with Charlotte in Bucks County, doing all the discount shops, going to the Playhouse, taking that mule-drawn ride on the canal with everyone sitting around on deck chairs on an open barge while the colonial homes of Bucks County passed in stately succession.

They were at the turning point on the canal ride—time to attach the mules to the other end and return to where they had come from—when she said to Charlotte, "What are you going to do when you retire?" Charlotte was a year younger, so she had an extra year to decide. It was odd, in a way, that they had never discussed this before.

"I've put my name on the list for Haven Homes," Charlotte said. "I want to go while I'm still young enough to make the adjustment. What about you?" She brushed imaginary crumbs from her aqua linen suit.

Charlotte's answer startled her, brought a whiff of foreboding. "Already you're going to Haven Homes?"

"I've put in for an apartment," Charlotte said. "That way I'll have the security when I need it. Consider coming out here, why don't you?"

"Thank you." She had been quite moved at Charlotte's suggestion. "That would be such a major move for me—Harrisburg to New Hope."

"Well, think about it," Charlotte said. "There might be an opening on the list if you act quickly. They're building some new apartments, and I don't think they're all spoken for yet."

She did think about it. But it was such a serious move, and it was hard to foresee just how it would turn out. It might be pleasant now, but in five years? Or ten?

She discussed it with her brother over the phone. Or rather, she described it to him. Before he had had a chance to respond she said, "I can't see my way clear to doing that now," and he said, "Okay."

"But I need to do something, Sammy," she said. She always called him Sammy when she needed some reassurance, some sense of caring family, somebody to bounce her quandaries against.

"If I were you, I'd take my time deciding," he advised. "You're financially set. Do you have hobbies you enjoy? Things you've wanted to do that you've had to put off? There must be a Senior Citizens' Center in Harrisburg."

"Busy work!" she said. "Flower arranging and bus trips to Gettysburg! Still, I don't want to just flounder around. You know I've always been a pretty systematic person."

"Don't I ever!" he said. "If you hadn't nagged me through it, I'd never have earned all those Boy Scout badges."

Tears sprang to her eyes. "Was I such a monster, Sam?" she asked, feeling somehow under attack.

"No, sweetheart. I'm glad I earned the badges. You were a pretty stern taskmaster though; I'll say that."

To myself, too, she thought. She didn't say anymore about it to him, but after they hung up she thought back over the long succession of years and how, with their mother and father always so busy making ends meet for the family, it had been she, the oldest daughter, who had fixed the meals, kept the house going, seen to it that the little children had clean clothes to wear, monitored their arguments. "So I've been so . . . *responsible!*" she said and ground her fist into her palm and straightened the doily under the plant and went and looked out the window.

Well, maybe she hadn't been the most spontaneous person in the world, but it had stood them all in good stead. The children had all gotten through college. When their parents died, first her father and two years later her mother—both of heart attacks, though her mother had lingered on after her first heart attack and she, Rebecca, had managed to care for her and teach school without missing a day—she had guided the family through all the estate settlement and property disposition without anyone apparently feeling slighted or losing their cool.

That was the problem. She was so used to schedules and plans that now, when she had some freedom, she didn't know what to do with it.

She kept reading ads in the paper. Not for jobs—she didn't want that. Travel notices? Special events? She read of a rally of a group called "Loners on Wheels"—single people who had travel trailers and converged on campgrounds for a week or two. Such apparent lightheartedness intrigued her, but she couldn't imagine doing such a thing. Well, maybe it would be fun to rent a travel trailer and do that once or twice. The thought of it lifted her to her feet, and she strode across her living room with a light heart until she saw herself in the mirror and thought, *You? You've never done a thing like that. Besides, you'd go, and then you'd come home and face the same problem of "What Do I Do With My Life Now?"*

Her church had a tutoring program for neighborhood children after school. She thought about getting involved in that; she was eminently qualified, after all. But she didn't want to do it all the time—after all, that was what she had retired from, after forty-five years.

"Go on some more cruises," a teacher friend suggested. "They have singles cruises. You might find a man." Rebecca wasn't amused. She had no wish to find a man. But she laughed, to be polite.

"Join an exercise class," friends recommended. "Take a course." "Sign up for volunteer work." Until she was dizzy from suggestions. One day, in desperation, she made a list of all the things either she had thought of herself to do with her newly acquired time or that well-meaning people had suggested to her. Just looking at it tired her out. Still, she wished something would help her decide—some sign from God—like sky-writing that used to trail over the stadium at high school football games—except this one would say, "Rebecca, here's what you should do. . . ."

She was out driving one Saturday afternoon the following spring after her retirement, when, passing through the rolling hills of Central Pennsylvania she came to a sign saying "Jumble Sale." Under the sign was an old metal washtub that would do nicely for some flowers she had been forcing and wanted to move outside. She hardly ever stopped at roadside sales, but this time she pulled over and got out.

A young girl stood at the improvised counter made from green-painted wooden boards resting on two sawhorses. She was wearing denim overalls and a white waffle-weave tee shirt. Her long yellow hair hung loose over her shoulders, and her eyes were a blue so pale you had to look twice to see the color at all.

"I'm interested in the washtub," she said and stooped over to pick it up and turn it to be sure there were no rusted-out spots. "How much is it?"

"Four dollars," the girl said.

She paid her and was about to leave, but then decided she was in no hurry, after all—a fact of which she had repeatedly to remind herself—and might as well look around.

It was then that she saw the quilt, hanging over a frame—reds and browns and blues and creams in random design, its seams laced with white featherstitching. Her mother had had a quilt like that; they kept it for best, used it only in the guestroom. Rebecca remembered—she hadn't thought of it in years (the quilt had gone to Janet)—how they used to pore over it, asking her mother for the identity of each piece. Many of them her mother didn't know about, but a few she recalled as scraps from a festive gown, a piece of family upholstery, or a scrap from an otherwise worn-out bureau scarf. There was even a piece of paisley from India, brought by her mother's cousin who for years had been a missionary in that exotic land.

At any rate, the sight of the quilt brought back a flood of memories of some rare times when her mother wasn't too busy to talk with her and of the cozy feelings that adhered to the memory of the guestroom, the old spool bed, the antique walnut chest that even now stood by her bed at home. She smoothed her hand over the quilt as it lay folded across a rack braced against a tree. "How much is this?" she asked.

"Fifty dollars," the girl said.

"Fifty dollars! Is it terribly worn?" She lifted it up, unfolded it. There were a few broken seams, a thread hanging here and there, but it seemed in good condition. She didn't need it; she had plenty of blankets at home. But she hadn't realized how much she missed that old quilt. While this wasn't the same, of course, it was close enough to be—well, a cousin, anyway.

"I'll take it," she said, and in a rare disclosure to a stranger, "My mother had a quilt like this. Is there a name to the pattern—I forget."

"Grandma?" said the girl and turned toward a shadowy figure seated under the edge of the shed. Rebecca hadn't seen that there was anyone there.

"It's a crazy quilt," came a voice. There was a rustle of fabric against chair, and a frail woman in a dress of blue homespun stepped out from under the roof of the shed. "A crazy quilt," she said again. "It's my prettiest one, but I've got a few others out back if you'd care to look."

Without waiting for an answer the woman started along a path toward the back of the white clapboard house and Rebecca followed, holding the quilt over her arm. *This is so unlike me,* she thought, feeling an unaccustomed lift of adventure, of the unknown, just in the simple act of following a stranger to a hidden place behind the house.

The woman sat down on a wood-slatted porch swing and motioned for Rebecca to sit beside her.

"See there," she said. On a worn wicker table were displayed at least a half-dozen other quilts—some of them in patterns of graduated stripes, alternating squares, radiating spokes. "Do you like any of them better?" the woman asked.

"Oh, no," Rebecca said. "I like this one. It reminds me of the one my mother had. But how do you follow the pattern for a quilt like this?"

The woman ran a gnarled hand over the quilt on Rebecca's lap. "Oh, you just do it," she said. "There isn't a pattern to this one—except, of course, you know what size you want, where your borders will be. You take one piece and add another piece on to it. Then another piece—it can go any which way."

"No pattern?" Rebecca echoed. "How do you know what you're doing?"

"That's the fun of it," the woman said, smiling and pushing gently against the ground with a worn, white tennis shoe. "The pieces tell you. Of course, you have some idea what you're making—a quilt, not a pillowcase. But the fun of a quilt like this is doing it a piece at a time and seeing how it turns out."

"It's beautiful. Imagine!" Rebecca mused, eyeing the way a square of brown velvet fit against a strip of calico and then against an uneven square of rose moiré taffeta. "I wonder if I could learn that?"

The woman looked surprised. "Well, I could get you started. But you'd have to find your own pieces." She reached down and pulled a woven basket piled high with scraps out from under the swing. "Here—choose a few," she said.

It was Rebecca's turn to be surprised. But then she thought, *Why not?* and lifted a piece of blue linen and one of flowered calico and a fragment of rose and cream homespun. "Will these do?"

"Of course. Whatever you choose." The woman took two of the pieces and began to sew them together. "You hitch 'em together like that," she said. She pulled a needle threaded with white embroidery cotton from the pincushion. "Then you feather over the seams. Like that," she said, holding it away from her. "It works out fine. You'd be surprised."

Rebecca watched intently as the woman attached the piece of homespun. "When you get these together, you choose the next piece," she said.

"Yes." Rebecca looked up at the green lawn—the apple trees fluttering in the late afternoon shifting of the wind. Across her field of vision a dark bird flew, and then another.

"There. That's it." The woman broke off the thread against her teeth and handed the pieced fabric to Rebecca. "Now see what you can do."

"I will. Believe me. I will." She lifted the quilt from her lap. "I'll be on my way. I can't thank you enough."

"Good luck. Just do it a piece at a time."

She found the young girl, paid for the quilt, put it in the wash-tub, loaded them both into her car, and drove off toward home, humming softly to herself.

On the way home she stopped at the deli. She never went there—all that rich food. Expensive, too. But on this late after-noon of her sign from God she bought herself some flowers and lobster salad and a furry kiwi fruit and a chocolate éclair.

When she reached home, she put the little quilt sample on her bureau. She had scraps of cloth and could easily find more if she ever wanted to make a quilt. But for now she would just keep it here, where she could see it every day.

She had dinner by the light of two blue candles and read for a while, then drew a warm bath and luxuriated in the bubbles and steam.

Then she spread the quilt on her bed, climbed in, and turned out the light. Staring into the friendly darkness, she thought about work and voyages and sewing projects and visits to the circus and helping with the tutoring at church and waiting to see how the wind blew across the multicolored, multishaped, wonderfully unordered patches of her life.

When the Lord brought us back to Jerusalem,
  it was like a dream!
How we laughed, how we sang for joy!

Psalm 126:1-2

TRIAL RUN

If Sharon and Kent hadn't been so sure, so absolutely positive, that she and Charlie would be much happier near them in Asheville than they could possibly be staying up in New England—"with those winters, Mother," Sharon would say (as though she'd not grown up there a perfectly healthy child with no more than the usual run of childhood diseases and an occasional common cold). If Sharon hadn't been so insistent, why, she and Charlie would never have agreed to move to Asheville at all, even for the trial run.

"We just want to take care of you, Mother," Sharon said, getting out the photos of "this darling little house," which turned out to be the least implicating residence in a retirement community just two miles from Sharon's and Kent's home. "The cottage has a wonderful view, too," Sharon said. "You and Dad can sit there and watch the sunset."

"We'll *be* the sunset," she had protested. "We're not interested in rocking our way in, feet first. Are we, Charlie?"

"No, we're not, Sylvie," he said. "Emphatically not."

They were down in the basement of their house in Wallingford when Sharon was, once again, making her pitch for them to move. Charlie was cleaning out what had been the coal bin in their first twenty years in the house. When they put in oil heat, they turned the coal bin into an extra fruit cellar—put shelves around the walls and a table in the middle for setting things down on when you came in. The children were still at home then; and one New Year's Eve, when everybody was getting over some bout with a mild flu so they couldn't go out and do anything celebrative, Sharon and Molly, who had probably been in ninth and seventh grade, had set up a "fruit room café" with candles stuck in old bottles and a tablecloth and chairs they dragged from somewhere. They had all four sat down there and drunk spiced grape juice and eaten fruitcake and sung "Auld Lang Syne" to see the New Year in.

It was one of her choicest memories of the house, along with the first birthday cake the girls had made for her—burned on the bottom and decorated with wilting violets from the back garden. And the endearing charade Molly had engaged in for a whole month one summer. She was probably four and just getting onto the concept of visiting. She would ring the front doorbell, and when Sylvia went to answer—Charlie was always at work, of course— she'd be standing there with her little plastic suitcase with the ballerina in white tutu painted on and she'd say, soberly, "My name is Molly. I've come to visit, and my mother said I could stay all night." Sylvia would open the door ceremonially and say, "How do you do, Molly? Won't you come in?" Or the time the girls had had a party, their first grown-up party, at the close of dancing school and Sharon had come into the kitchen in tears. "Nobody's dancing!" she wailed; and Charlie had thought up some silly pairing game that got them all dancing and cavorting and having a wonderful time, so that when eleven o'clock came and the parents began to come for their sons and daughters, no one wanted to leave. And even Billy Gammel, the hearthrob of ninth grade and the prize attendee, had said, "This is the most fun I ever had in my life!"— which left Sharon practically swooning with delight. Decades of memories in this house. And now Sharon wanted them to leave it.

The pressure to move south began before Charlie retired from his job as chief engineer at the power company. Sharon and Kent and the twins were there on a summer visit, and Molly flew up from Florida a few days early on her way to a bank meeting in New York. Sylvia couldn't tell whether there had been collusion on the girls' part before they got there, or whether Sharon had talked Molly into agreement after they'd been together a day or two. But they were all out on the back terrace and Charlie was sweating over a grill, cooking hamburgers. It had been a beastly hot day—one of those New England summer days when you pull the shades in the morning and by afternoon all you want to do is lie on the floor or sit in a hard chair with the electric fan blowing toward you over a bowl full of ice. She had thought there might be air moving outside, so she had suggested this cookout—though probably a cold tuna salad would have been better. Even the twins were a little slowed by the heat. They were twelve then and given to histrionic sighing. "It's so hot!" Barbie said and Bethie flopped her long braid and echoed, "You're telling me! I wish we had air conditioning."

A few people in Wallingford did have air conditioning, but Sylvia had always felt to have air conditioning just for those few dog days showed some kind of character weakness, especially in view of the need to conserve energy, to save the planet. Nor was Charlie, who probably could have gotten some kind of deal on equipment because of the power company, tempted. "How would we know it was summer if we were all cooped up in an icebox?" he said when, just once, she had tentatively sounded him out—"Now that we're getting older, maybe we should consider. . . ."

But Bethie's mention of air conditioning launched Molly into a speech about the pleasures of Asheville's moderate climate. "We do have air conditioning"—she nodded in her parents' direction, acknowledging she knew their stand on the matter—"but our utility bills over the year are much lower than yours, I'm sure. And, as you get older"—she hesitated—"Well, not now, but in a few years, you may find these extremes of climate harder to take."

It was about half an hour after that—one hamburger apiece and hot dogs for those who wanted them and some of her famous potato salad, though she had swapped yogurt for the mayonnaise these last few years—that Sharon said, looking toward Molly for corroboration, so you knew they had talked about it, "When you retire, Dad, think about moving to Asheville? It's a lovely climate, and I'm sure we could find you a nice place near us. Closer to Florida, too, so Molly could come up. A lot of older people are moving there, so there's a lot going on for"—again she had the grace to hesitate—"senior citizens."

She looked at Charlie. She could tell he was not smitten by the idea—but touched, as she was, by the suggestion. "No, thanks, dear," he said. "We've been here a long time, and I suppose we'll stay." It *was* dear of Sharon, but Sylvia had to admit, too, to a lingering sense of disappointment that, having grown up here, the girls could dismiss so blithely the holding power of this place. Though she was glad they weren't tied to it. You could be imprisoned by a place, by your dependence on it, and she knew that.

But you could also be freed by its very *givenness* in your life—the familiarity of it leaving you free to take on all kinds of adventures, so long as you knew you could come home.

A year and a half later, Charlie retired. The power company had a big party for him. The girls came up, and there were pictures for the paper. When Charlie was asked about retirement plans, he said, "We plan to stay right here—at least for a while."

In her letters and phone calls Sharon would tell them how wonderful life was in Asheville—so close to the mountains and yet milder in winter. They had been to visit the Biltmore and could hardly wait to take Sylvia and Charlie when they came down— "such a healthful climate," Sharon wrote. They would take them to visit Thomas Wolfe's house too. But mostly it was climate, and being close together so they could see a lot of each other. "Kind of keep track," was the way Sharon put it.

"I'm not sure I want her 'keeping track,'" Sylvia told Charlie. "Now that we're retired I feel a whole new burst of carefreeness coming on. Know what I mean?"

He smiled at her. "Right. We maintained our sober demeanor long enough, raising our respectable family, being solid citizens. Let's go to the amusement park."

It was a beautiful spring day, and the amusement park had just opened for the season. When they got there, the attendants were still taking the dull green covers off the Dodgem cars, rolling the canvas curtains up over the concession stands. "I still don't want to go on the roller coaster," Sylvia said. "I never have. But I'd like the merry-go-round. How about it?" So they went on the merry-go-round and on the boats in the pond and even on the Dodgem, banging against the wide rubber bumper and clattering back onto the crowded floor, ricocheting off other cars (unoccupied) while the trolley above them swayed with the impact of their jerking antennae.

She wrote Sharon about it, and Molly. "Dad and I had a wonderful day at the park. Next week the zoo."

The girls were tolerantly amused. But when they learned their parents were planning a short hike on the Appalachian Trail and had bought snowshoes and that Charlie had bought himself a full set of electric trains, they were not so forebearing. It was Christmastime when he showed them. "I always wanted a train set, but we couldn't afford it. And when you girls were young—at that time it didn't seem the right toy for girls," he said, apologetically. "Watch this!" And he flicked a switch and lights went on and the engine started chugging through the artificial snow, wending its way among cottages and fire department and city hall.

"Dad!" Molly said. "Don't you think you've overdone it?"

But the last straw was when Sharon came for a visit one winter and got in a few hours earlier than she had expected and stepping out of the taxi saw her mother in snow pants and hooded snow jacket, lying on her back on a patch of fresh snow and sweeping her arms in arcs through the snow to make outlined "angel wings."

"Mother!" she exclaimed and paid the taxi driver as though the whole thing embarrassed her, though the driver chuckled, "Have a nice day!" with more than usual élan as he drove away.

After that the campaign to move was stepped up—brochures from the Chamber of Commerce, announcements of the meetings of community literary and garden clubs and chess clubs, and golf courses where you could "Play 12 months out of 12."

"Especially with the girls going, Mother—I'll have lots of time to be with you." Sylvia experienced a slight waft of chill air going by her as she heard this a thousand miles away on the phone. Because more and more, she was relishing time to herself, time to be with Charlie—to do some of the foolish things they had had neither the time nor the freedom from the staid proprieties of adulthood to do when they were parents of growing children or Charlie had his professional image to maintain.

But life got harder in Wallingford. The screens became more of a chore each year. And Sylvia's arthritis didn't do as well in damp spring or cold winter. Their friends, too, began to fail, and a few of them died.

So one spring, after a particularly harsh winter, they rented out their house—"No lease, just a month at a time, until we see how we like it," Charlie told the young accountant who moved in with his wife and year-old baby—and took up residence in a garden apartment in a complex two miles down the road from Sharon and Kent. The complex was geared to "multi-level senior housing"— which meant as residents got more and more frail they moved to facilities providing increasing levels of care. Sylvia and Charlie were in their own unit now, but the shadow of the hospital unit lay over their back cement patio every afternoon while they were sitting out at Sharon's urging "to enjoy the view of the mountains."

The twins were seventeen by now and about to leave for college in the midwest. The summer was busy, getting them outfitted and getting Sylvia and Charlie settled in their house and acquainted with the community.

Sylvia was in no hurry to have every domestic item in place right away, but, particularly after the girls left for college, Sharon seemed to take it on as a cause. She had lived in her own house now for twenty years and, short of starting over on a complete redecorating project, there was nothing that needed doing.

So she took on Sylvia and Charlie's as her own—bringing swatches for drapes and bedspreads, pushing the furniture around to get the most pleasing effect, deciding where to put the blue Japanese vases and how best to display the water color of Mount Katahdin.

Kent, too, with his daughters gone, was only too happy to take Charlie golfing and help plant bushes in the yard. "It's a whole different growing pattern here, Dad," he said, shoving the point of his shovel into the ground. "You don't have to worry about deep freezing."

"Do you have arbutus?" Charlie asked.

"Oh, no—we don't have most of those northern wildflowers. We have lovely crepe myrtle in the summer."

"I suppose," Charlie said, not having the least idea what crepe myrtle was.

He had never been that keen on golfing, either—considering it a sport of somewhat decadent non-athletes, who rode around in those carts mulling over which of their expensive sticks to try next, and called that exercise.

And, of course, they saw all the sights—took long drives east into the edge of the Smokies, went to the Biltmore, visited the home of Thomas Wolfe and when the guide mentioned Wolfe's famous "literary masterpiece *You Can't Go Home Again*," Sylvia winced and looked at the wall with its faded, flowered paper.

Molly came up from Florida for Thanksgiving. She was just as tan as she had been in the summer. It hadn't bothered Sylvia when they lived in Connecticut, but somehow, drifting closer to the South herself, it jarred her sense of the natural order to have her daughter tan in the winter.

The trees were green for Thanksgiving, too, and there wasn't a trace of cold in the air—let alone the predictive snow that sometimes fell in the woods behind their house during that last week in November.

In fact, it wasn't cold at all. Oh, as the winter progressed, it did get down to freezing a few times, and they had what they called a snowstorm—which was an inch of snow on the ground that closed the schools for a week because they had no snow removal equipment. Though the snow was long gone from the town streets, the buses that traveled the back roads might still encounter a dangerous patch of slick ice.

Still, Sharon and Kent were so solicitous. "Are you warm enough? Can you adjust your thermostats right? Why don't you come over Saturday? Dad and Kent can play golf, and Mother and I can watch a movie. Then we can all have supper together. We'll get you home in plenty of time for a good night's sleep. We'll come and get you for church in the morning—How's that?"

Until one day Sylvia and Charlie looked at one another and acknowledged it—they didn't like it here. Not at all. Life in Asheville was too moderate for people who had grown up living in extremes of temperature. The retirement village, too, was too easy. "No challenge of wood to cut for the fireplace. Or strawberry canes to scratch your pants. Or flowers you have to protect over the winter."

"I feel smothered, almost, too," Sylvia said, with tears in her eyes because she felt so guilty, saying anything against the daughter and son-in-law who were trying to take such good care of them.

"The thing is, I want to take care of myself. And you, Charlie. I want to take care of you. I want baked beans and fish chowder. They don't even have a Boston cracker in the store."

"And I want to take care of you, Sweetheart," Charlie said, getting up from his bent hickory rocker with more alacrity than she had seen in his step for four months and coming over to plant a firm kiss on the top of her head. "I hate golf. I want to go back to hiking while we're able. I love Kent, but he's gotten too slowed-down, too Southern for my taste." And he went and stood in front of the painting of Mount Katahdin and drew a long deep breath. "Sometimes we need our own mountains," he said.

They called up their renters and told them that when the next month's rent ran out, they would be coming back. "Oh, that's too bad," the nice accountant said. "We were really liking it here—though the wind is blowing pretty hard down the chimney tonight."

"Exactly," Charlie said, and when he hung up, that's what he told Sylvia. "The wind is blowing hard down the chimney, Sylvie," he said.

"I can't wait," she said.

So the next time Sharon and Kent came over, bringing a chess pie and a bowl of gumbo, they thanked them very much and after they had all enjoyed supper together, Sylvia said, "Children?"

"Yes," Sharon said, looking up from the tablecloth from which she was carefully brushing a few crumbs onto a plastic receiver held just below the table edge. Kent was obviously attentive, too.

"Your father and I are very grateful for all your care in bringing us down here. You've done everything to make us welcome, to make it easy for us. But. . . ." She looked at Charlie because she didn't know how to put it and maybe he would know.

"It's too easy, that's the problem," Charlie said. "It's not what we're used to, and we're going home."

Kent and Sharon looked at each other, then back at Sylvia and Charlie. Sharon's eyes filled with tears. "But why?" she said. "I thought we were all doing well together."

"We have done well together," Sylvia said. "And we're grateful to you and Kent. But for a while at least, Dad and I will do better back home."

It took them a month to collect their things and pack them up and ship them off. It wasn't easy to say goodbye to the children. "You'll see," Sylvia said. "You'll be fine. Give yourself a little time. And thanks for everything."

Charlie hugged his daughter. "Bye, dear," he said, his voice gruff.

Ten miles out of town Sylvia said, "Oh, I hope we did the right thing.

"I'm sure we did," Charlie said. "I'm already tasting that fish chowder." When they got back to Wallingford and pulled into their driveway once more, they knew they were home.

At the end of the spring, Sharon and Kent came up to see them. Yes, the girls were fine. They had been home for midterm, and it was nice to have them but fine to send them off again, too.

"You'll be down next winter to see us, won't you?" Sharon asked shyly, as though fearful of touching an old wound.

"Oh, yes, we'll be ready for some southern sunshine by then," Sylvia said.

And in celebration of weathering another crisis, the four of them took off for the amusement park, which had just barely opened for the season, so there was hardly anyone there. "Thank heavens!" Sharon said. "At our age!"

"Who cares anyway?" Charlie said.

They went on the merry-go-round, and the Dodgem, and this time when they got to the roller coaster, Sylvia said, "I think I'd like to go on this one. I never have. You know—a trial run."

They all stepped into the first carriage and, hanging on for dear life, off they went, the machine chugging, screeching, and roaring, up and down, up and down, until, dizzy and breathless, they ended up on the level track once more.

"Well, thank goodness!" Sylvia said as she climbed out onto the blessed ground. "That's all. For this time, at least."

You are no longer strangers and sojourners, but you are fellow citizens with the saints and members of the household of God.

Ephesians 2:19 (RSV)

THE GIFT

At four o'clock, when the church kitchen was cleaned up and the custodian had taken the garbage out and they had said goodbye to the last of the volunteers—"Thanks. See you next time."—Maria Prescott went to collect her purse from the back of the broom closet, only to find that it wasn't there.

She stared at the closet wall, at the black double hooks with string-handled dustpans, at the brass-colored brackets for used paper bags, at the shelf with its scouring powders and layered trays. Where was her purse? She had hung it there, safely behind the dingy coat sweaters, an old rain slicker, the bag of clothespins left over from the days when anyone hung clothes out on a line— the same place she had put it each Tuesday and Friday since she had taken over doing the cooking, and supervising the church's program for feeding the street people two hot meals a week. The purse wasn't there. Could one of the volunteers have picked it up, thinking it was hers? No. They all put their purses where they could keep their eye on them—in the cupboard by the sink, where they got in the way of detergents and dish drainers. "Put them where I leave mine," she invited them, indicating the small broom closet. "No one ever goes there."

But someone must have, because her purse was gone.

My wallet, she thought. *My license. My credit cards. My pictures of my family.*

Frantic, she pulled the white-painted drawers out in quick succession, then slammed them closed. Her purse couldn't be in there—it was too big. Perhaps someone had accidentally picked it up, hooked it on a button of a coat, not realizing? She bent to look under the tables, pulled out the bins of sugar and flour. Of course, it wasn't there.

She closed the closet door and leaned against it, a hollow feeling in her chest, like a pain. She saw in her mind's eye the rows of tables and chairs in the community room, the ragged discards of Nashville—men, an occasional woman and child—seated at the tables with silverware and vases of flowers. On their plates no doctored-up canned foods passing for homemade. She always insisted they be given fresh food—slices of ham basted with pineapple-mustard sauce, sweet potatoes cozied with orange sections, fresh green beans with just a little of the ham flavor, green salad with sliced mushrooms and green onions and the sweet-sour dressing made from her mother's recipe. Usually they didn't come into the kitchen, though over here at the end of the room a person could have slipped in and out without being noticed.

She heard the swish of a broom across the tile floor in the community room. It was Will, sweeping up. She hated to let him know. He had been skeptical of this venture at the beginning—"You let those folks in here, you can't count on what could happen. Besides, think of the bugs." They had all appreciated his pride in keeping the church clean, and maybe if she had had to dump the extra disinfectant over everything and watch for lice in the coat room she would have felt the same. But he had been won over, had even become friendly with some of the regulars. "How're you doing, Bud?" to Bud Bakersfield, who looked as though a slight wind or even a rush of air through the door would blow him over.

"Just fine, Will," Bud would answer.

And "Where's Sully?" he had asked the first Friday Sully wasn't there. When Maria had told him the good news about Sully returning to his family, Will had grinned and clomped his broom down on the floor. "Well, is that a fact?" he said.

But now, to tell him there had been a theft.

"Did you see any strangers come into the kitchen this morning, Will?" she asked.

"No, ma'am," he said. "Just the regulars."

"You've been here all the time, haven't you?"

"Every minute, Miss Maria. Something wrong?"

She hesitated, but then decided she might as well tell him. "My purse is missing, Will."

He stopped his sweeping, mid-stroke, as incredulous—she hoped that was what his expression meant—as she had been. Then he closed his mouth, tight-lipped, and turned away. "Coulda' told you," he said.

She went back into the kitchen and sat on one of the stools and stared at the trash barrel full of cans piled in precarious balance, plastic milk bottles crushed to awkward opaque saucers, and crumpled paper towels. *Some of those things could be recycled*, she thought. In the rush of getting the meal ready they sometimes neglected to put the various kinds of trash in the separate bins. On the wall by the freezer hung a plaque someone had done in calligraphy and decorated with trailing green leaves and budded white flowers. "Peace to all who enter here," it said. Beside that was a framed quotation from Brother Lawrence about possessing God as surely in the kitchen as on his knees at the Blessed Sacrament.

Well, maybe, Maria thought and closed her eyes against the hollowness in her chest. How could someone have taken her purse, knowing one another as they did? She had sailed into this work, determined to be a sister, a mother, determined that she could love these men into trusting—and the several women who came, too, though there seemed already a bond between women that made it easier. She had often said it—maybe, she wondered now, to convince herself it was true—"People become trustworthy by being trusted." It was her version of the old Danish proverb she loved, except that it was sexist and elitist, speaking of kings as it did. But it was still a good thought: "In every man there is a king. Speak to the king and the king will come forth." That was what she had determined to do here—against the sensible wisdom of Ariel and Stewart. "Mother, at your age, you deserve some rest."

"Later," she had said. "I ain't no ways tired"—quoting the old saying handed down from the slaves. She would never use that language with a white person, but with her own daughter. . . .

"Mother!" Ariel protested. She didn't know whether at the reminder of slave days or at the impossibility of her mother, at almost eighty, not being tired.

Maria had recently retired from Tuskegee Institute when she came to Nashville on an extended visit with her daughter, and almost before she knew it she had gotten embroiled in the life of Rosedale church.

She had gone to the church partly just to clear her head. She'd been in Nashville three weeks, visiting Ariel and her family and then staying on the week Ariel went on tour with her dance company.

Then Ariel came back, and they had all had a good visit, and it was time she was heading home. To Lucinda, who followed her from room to room, who burst in from kindergarten each day with the question, "Grandma, where are you?" she had made a promise to come back in a few months.

But for now she would like to get home. Life in Ariel's household was more strenuous than in her own cozy brick house on the edge of the Tuskegee campus, to which she had moved twenty years ago, when Ralph died and left her with two teenagers. They hadn't needed the big house out by the river and besides, it was a comfort being on the edge of the campus. So many of her friends were associated with Tuskegee one way or another and she could walk to her job in the personnel office and then—so she reasoned at the time—Jimmy and Ariel could go to Tuskegee and live right there at home but still feel close to campus life. Besides, she'd had her fill of riding on buses. Sometimes, going to those rallies in Montgomery or Birmingham or to registration campaigns in small Alabama towns, she could have gotten a ride in someone's car but she would take the bus to prove the point: she was as entitled as anyone else to sit wherever there was an empty seat.

As it turned out, Ariel didn't go to Tuskegee. "I want to be a dancer, Mom," she had said. "I want to go to New York. If I start to dance down here this is where I'll stay. Besides, look here"—and she took from her zippered notebook a catalog from Sarah Lawrence, with a photograph of Martha Graham and another of José Limón leaping across a black-grained bare stage. "I have to see them to know what I can do." She had gotten a scholarship to Sarah Lawrence, and when she got through she'd danced with the Martha Graham Dance Company. Maria had gone up and sat in the darkened theater among strangers and wept with astonishment and joy and wished—oh, how she had wished—that Ralph could have been here to see his daughter, diaphanous and beautiful, graceful as a water fountain, balanced against the outstretched arm of a blond male dancer. And the program notes didn't say a thing about who was black and who was white.

When she got back to the tiny apartment Ariel shared with two other women, Maria called Jimmy in Anniston. He was a shop teacher then, and a basketball coach. "You would have been proud of your sister," she said. "That's great!" he said. "Guess what? Wanda and I are going to be married."

Ariel and Stewart met at Jimmy's wedding. He and Jimmy had been classmates at Tuskegee, and Stewart had gone on to law school. As soon as he finished, he and Ariel were married in the Tuskegee chapel and they moved to Nashville. Ariel had her children and in between kept up with her dancing as best she could. Just now, at thirty-six, she was eager to devote more time to her career. But, of course, Lucinda was still only five. Wouldn't it be nice if Maria—it was a suggestion only and they didn't want to push her—but wouldn't it be nice if Maria came to live with them, or maybe, if she didn't want to live right in with them, in an apartment nearby?

That was one reason Maria had gone, not to church with Ariel and Stewart and the children, but to this other church she had heard about—an interracial church, near a university, with white folks and black folks, poor folks and middle-class folks. She needed some church time alone, time to think. If she came here, she didn't want to get swallowed up in Ariel's and Stewart's life, not completely. Besides, she was a veteran of the Civil Rights struggle, and she was curious to see what the church was like.

She had gone to hear Martin Luther King, Jr. in Montgomery, taking a pencil and pad so she could pretend to be a member of the press and sit up close. The first time Church Women United planned to have a mixed-race meeting and at first only the light-skinned women were going, she had said, "Nobody'll know you're not a white woman. I'm coming, too," and she had taken toothbrush and comb and extra underwear because she was so sure she would get arrested and wanted to be ready. She had joined the bus trip for the March on Washington when she was fifty-four years old. She had watched the Civil Rights movement spread like dandelion seeds through the colleges and universities and then through the segregated brotherhoods and sisterhoods and into the churches— though some of the churches sang about heaven, my home, and for a long time would have preferred to look the other way. There was enough trouble in the world already. Why try to make everything over when chances were you would just get your feelings smashed and maybe worse than that?

But maybe then, she had thought, *she would like to take it easy for a while—travel some, read, work in her garden, visit her children and grandchildren.* "I've worked hard for fifty years," she would say, giving herself a generous fifteen years of childhood. "I'm ready for a rest."

She had settled into her little house and begun to have lunch with friends and go to antique shows and read some of the books that had piled up. She wondered about taking a course in quilting or painting or needlepoint—except that those tiny squares in the canvas made her eyes tired.

Then one day she had had the letter from Ariel. "Mom, I may get to go on a summer dance tour to Europe. Any chance you could come for a visit?"

She had gone the next week, and the invitation to visit became an invitation to stay.

The church, when she found it, didn't look like a church. It looked like a house, and it was. The congregation sat on folding chairs in a big room that had been expanded from a two-car garage. On the painted cement-block walls hung posters that said, "Truth comes in bits and pieces" and "Not to decide is to decide" and "Ships in a harbor are safe, but that's not what ships are for," and she thought, *Well—ships do need harbors, too*; and she was tired and thought, *I'd like a harbor for a while.* But then she saw a banner of black and white felt, and the words on it were "Let my people go!" and she thought, *Well, maybe.*

They had a time for announcement of prayer concerns, and somebody told of visiting a friend in prison and someone else told of agitating for better street-lighting in the housing projects and a better bus schedule and she thought, *This feels like home.*

She saw a black man and a white woman and a fidgety child who was obviously their child, and someone beside them reached over and gave him a crayon and a pad to scribble on, and she thought, *That's good.* Some children were introduced who were part of the church's after-school program and they read a play they had written in one of the classes. It was very short, about some birds that were sharing the birdbath and kept knocking each other off the rim— until a cat came along; then they decided they could both use the birdbath after all. The congregation laughed and clapped when they were finished. Then they all stood to sing and a fidgety razor-thin white man who seemed to have a kind of a tic on one side of his face held out to her an open songbook and on the other side stood a black man with a salt and pepper beard and they sang together, "Lift every voice and sing, till earth and heaven ring,/ring with the harmonies of liberty."

At the end of the sermon, when an invitation was given for any-one who wanted to unite with this congregation, it was as if God directly attached some string to her heart and said, "This is where you belong. Come, my daughter. Come." And she got up and walked from her creaky folding chair in the third row of creaking chairs set up around three sides of the sanctuary and went forward. "I just came as a visitor," she said, and the minister, a balding white man with freckles climbing into his thinning hair, set down his Bible and his service book and put his arms around her, and she joined, right then and there.

Ariel was surprised. Stewart was irate. "If you're going to join a church, go with us, not with those white folks with their Uncle Toms."

"Hush," she said. "I don't want Lucinda hearing that kind of talk."

For a while she limited her presence in the church to Sunday services, and then she joined the adult Sunday school class and then she began to go to the women's meetings. With Ariel's help she found an apartment midway between Ariel's house and the church. She kept her house in Tuskegee—who knew when she might decide to go back? She wrote regularly to her old group of friends. Sometimes she would get on the bus and go back for a visit, or they would come to see her.

"What you doing in a church like that?" some of them would say. "After all we went through, how come you don't stay with the brothers and sisters?" they would ask.

There were times when she wondered the same thing, times such as one day in the Sunday school class, when one of the young men told about having to leave his childhood black friend behind when he went away to school. "I complied, too," the young man said, his blue-gray eyes pained at his own capitulation back then.

"Well, have you gone back and found him?" Maria asked.

"No, I haven't, Maria." He was apologetic, but it wasn't enough. She cried and left the room. When she saw the young man later after church, she apologized. "I'm sorry I made a scene over that. It's just that. . . ." And she wondered again, *Do I really belong in a church like this?*

But when the feeding program began—this church taking its turn along with other churches at feeding the homeless, even sending the church bus clear downtown to pick up the ones who gathered around the W.C.T.U. water fountain by the bus station— and they needed somebody to organize the work and supervise the cooking, she took it on for a while. "I'm almost eighty years old," she said. "I can't do it for long."

But she found she liked it, and folks from lots of churches— white churches—would come to help, and every day they would all don their aprons and work along beside each other. It made her feel good, made her feel like the best of those days when the white students had come south to help with registration, and they had stood together registering voters, and at the end of the day they joined in a circle of crossed arms and swaying together they sang, "We Shall Overcome" and believed it, for a while at least.

At first, the street people were withdrawn, shy. They would never look you in the eye. They would eat, pass their plates back for seconds (she insisted on real plates, even before the cry went up of no paper plates for ecology's sake), mutter their thanks, finish their food, wipe their beard-stubbled faces, line up for the dingy bathroom, and file back out the door and onto the bus without ever having looked you in the eye.

She had put an end to that. Every morning before she began work she prayed for them, prayed for herself, prayed for the other workers who would be coming. As she began to know whom to expect, she would hold each of those shabby, downward-looking men before the Lord and say, "Today. Let them know today that we love them. Because that's how they're going to know you love them. And if they know folks love them, then they'll be able to look us in the eye and not shuffle around and pretend they don't see who we are."

And bit by bit the men had changed. "Howdy, Miss Maria," they would say when they came in the door. "Sure like that pretty dress you're wearin'." They began to bring her tattered photographs of families they had left behind somewhere. She would sit them down and pull a chair up beside them and look at the pictures like they were pictures of God Almighty. "Tell me about this lady," she'd say, and she'd listen and listen and listen. And once or twice one of the men would take a notion to save up the pittance of money he had gotten and go back home. Sully Watkins even wrote her a letter telling how he had gone back to Huntsville and gotten a job and he was living with his "old lady" and he hadn't had anything to drink since he got there—"Because of you, Miss Maria," he wrote. "That's what made me strong to do it."

That day she made such a mess dishing up the banana pudding that Sue Miller had to take over and do it for her. "What's the matter, Maria?" Sue asked, laughing. "You need new glasses or something?"

"No," she said. "I'm so happy thinking about Sully being home and sober I just can't keep my mind on banana pudding."

It wasn't only Sully, either. Tom Hollowfield, who when he first came would always get up and move if she sat down at the table next to him; and once she heard him mutter, "I ain't eatin' with no niggers," one day brought her a piece of goldenrod he'd found along the railroad track. "A flower for you," he said and she had put it in a vase on the table.

When Stewart took a job in El Paso and the family urged her to move with them, she said, no, her church family was here now and she guessed she would stay. When she thought *church family*, she thought of those people who came to eat with her on Tuesday and Friday as well as the members of the congregation.

So now she had invested them with family-ness, her own rescued kin—and how could one of them have stolen her purse?

She told the balding white minister about her loss. Grief and anger suffused his face. "We'll replace the money," he said. "Did you stop payment on your credit cards?"

"I will," she said.

"But it won't stop the hurt," he said.

"No," she said.

At home, she thought of their faces. There had been no new people in that Friday lunch gathering. In her mind she paraded them before herself, stood them in a row, like a police line-up, looked into their eyes. Tom? Archie? Bruno? Maylynne? Rocky? Sam? Who could it have been? The fact of the theft hung heavy in her chest—solid, immovable, like an enclosed cyst, a coconut, hard-shelled and dark. If she could break into it, if she could scream, or cry, maybe she would feel better. It took up so much room in her chest she wondered how she was able to breathe. It didn't do any good to ask herself why she was so upset. With all she'd seen in her lifetime, why such a fuss about someone stealing a purse? Probably whoever took it needed the little money in it worse than she did. She shook her head, unconvinced. *Maybe I'm too old*, she thought. *Something like this I just can't handle anymore.*

Two days later, the mailman, walking down the street, found her purse beside a tree. The money was gone from her wallet, along with her credit cards. Her license and the accordion plastic sleeves of her photos were still there. One by one she looked over the faces of her grandchildren, angered at what had been a violation of them as well.

Over the next weeks, she steeled herself not to look into the eyes of each of the lunch people, wondering, *Was it you?* There were no dropouts to indicate that maybe a guilty conscience had exacted its penalty.

Each Tuesday and Friday before she went to the church, she prayed that this betrayal would not arm her against the guests who would be coming on the bus. When she heard the brakes squeak and the bus grind to a halt, she prayed again from the window, "They are your people. They are Christ in disguise"—even as she acknowledged with a wry inner smile that the disguise was pretty effective.

Still, there was a lump in her chest that would not go away, would not dissolve; and her vigilance against resentment could still catch her off guard and she would find herself wanting them to be gone—the connection between herself and these destitute of the city perfunctory and untended. And sometimes when it came time to dish up the beans or the beef stew, she would hand her spoon over to one of the volunteers and say, "Could you do this? I've been on my feet awhile," and she'd go and put dishes away or do something where she didn't have to look at the men's faces as they went by.

When she got another letter from Ariel in El Paso, not long before Christmas, saying, "Mother, I've been offered a place in the Company. I'd have to travel about one week a month. Are you ready to think about retiring again? There's a wonderful little house just across the street from us," she sat on the edge of her bed and saw herself in Ariel's lovely blue-and-white kitchen, the pot of marigolds on the windowsill, the chair where Lucinda would sit her down and climb up in her lap and talk with her about school. Then Lucinda would say, "Tell me what it was like when you were little. What kind of shoes? What kind of dresses? What kind of books did you read?" and they would rock and hold one another, and she would think, *This is the blessing of age, this child against my breast*. She thought of the church and the palpable love she had felt there and how, with the theft of her purse, it had lost some of its luster. And yes, she was tired. She couldn't continue to work here indefinitely.

But she couldn't leave now. The Christmas season was only half over, and it was hard to get volunteers to help in December. They had planned a special Christmas dinner for December 20, and after that she would go.

She wrote out a letter of resignation and put it in her purse. She didn't trust herself to say goodbye to the minister and the people. Perhaps it was cowardly, but maybe she had earned the right to a quiet departure, with no fanfare.

She wrote back to Ariel. "I'm thinking about it. But at present I'd like to come as soon as we've had our Christmas dinner here."

The day of the dinner she went bright and early, hung up her coat and her purse in the same closet from which it had been stolen, and closed the door. Her letter of resignation was in the purse. She would put it on the minister's desk and leave. She could already feel the lightness in her step as she walked away from here, but there was dejection also; the hurt still weighed her down.

The dinner was over. The last of the pumpkin pie had been eaten and the dishes were being cleared away when she was aware, from her place at one side of one of the long tables, of a stirring along the row. Before the theft she had always insisted on being in the middle of a table and though she had felt like retreating—even eating in the kitchen away from the street people—she had thought it would be conspicuous, so she stayed. "I want to be part of the action," she had said, and laughed, knowing she had fallen way behind in whatever the current street phrases were.

The men were looking at her, then looking quickly away. Could they tell? Was there something in her countenance to give away her secret—that this was to be her last time? Had she failed in her effort to be loving, accepting—even though her heart twisted at the thought of someone's betrayal?

Now they were all looking toward Tom Hollowfield. He leaned

across the table, his hand veined with ground–in dirt, the cuff of his plaid flannel shirt dragging threads across an empty coffee cup. He whispered to Mike Satterly. They looked down the row. Then Tom pushed back his chair from the table and cleared his throat. "I want," he began.

"Go to the front," a couple of voices called out. Zoo Elkins pushed on Tom's elbow, forcing him into the corridor made by the rows of folding chairs.

"All right, all right," Tom said, and they all laughed, as though he had just told some engaging story. He had a paper bag in his hand.

He walked to the front of the room.

Maria looked around. No one else was moving. These men weren't given to lingering. And why was everyone so quiet?

"All right," Tom said again from his place in front of the big black and white banner. The group laughed again.

What's going on? Maria wondered.

"Miss Maria, would you come up here, please?" Tom asked, a smile creasing into his several days' growth of stubble. His arm in its dingy sleeve—the plaid all but obliterated by grime—reached out to beckon her forward.

She stood. All eyes were on her.

"Come on," Tom urged, as she appeared to hesitate.

She saw the rows of faces looking up like expectant, trusting children—though they bore the wrinkles and grime of the destitute, the wearing of age and ill fortune.

Tom was pulling something from the brown paper bag. It was a red-wrapped package tied with a gold string. She recognized the wrap—the Christmas gift wrap of the city's best downtown bookstore. There was a card on it, tucked under the gold cord.

Tom handed the package to her and cleared his throat. "We took up a collection," he said and looked conspiratorially at the rows of destitute men, their faces beaming now because how long had it been for any of them since they had put money in a collection to give something away? "And we bought this for you," he said, "because"—and here his voice faltered because what he wanted to say was not the language of men scrabbling for existence on the streets and grillworks of this city. He swallowed again, his Adam's apple a visible knot rising and falling in his scrawny bewhiskered throat, "because you love us so much," he said, at the end the words little more than a whisper.

But she heard. Oh, how she heard! She took the package from him. "Thank you"—her words, too, soft in the close-packed room. But they were listening; they could hear her heart beat—the echo of their own.

Reverently, she slipped off the cord and folded back the paper against black leatherette, with pages edged in shining gold. "A Bible," she breathed and held it against her breast and crossed her wrists over it and moaned. But it was a moan of gratitude, not sadness. It was a moan of letting go.

Because, almost as though it were a hot water bottle against a chunk of ice or a flash of laser light, the Bible against her chest had dissolved the lump of resentment and hurt that had been her constant companion these weeks since the theft, so that she could scarcely move without somehow accommodating to that heaviness in her life. It was gone, flashed away as with a beam of light.

Her eyes stung. "Thank you," she murmured and sat down. And put her hands to her face. And cried. At last. But there was laughter in her crying, too. And she looked around the room—up one aisle and down the next—and knew from somewhere deep inside herself that whether she went to Ariel's or whether she tore up the letter and stayed or whether she went back to her own house in Tuskegee—it didn't matter at all. Because, looking at those faces and that Bible she had held across her chest like a shield and buckler, she guessed that whoever had taken her purse that day— if that person was here, and he probably was—then he was sorry. Or even if all of them had done it—which she knew was not possi- ble—but even if they had colluded on some act of theft—why, they were all sorry. And some day, in the fullness of time, all the people from the street and from the city and all those she had loved and lost, and Martin Luther King, Jr., and her own Mama and Daddy and her beloved Ralph, who probably would never have understood why on earth she was doing what she was doing—any more than Ariel, beautiful and lithe in her dancing clothes, could probably make neither head nor tail out of it—they would all come together around tables like this (not with paper plates either); and the rights of everyone would be honored and the wrongs of every-one—even whoever it was who took her purse, even her own wrongs when she couldn't forgive—well, they wouldn't matter at all either.

Who could have guessed it? "Well, Lord have mercy," she said.

Photo: Peter Hickman

ABOUT THE AUTHOR

Martha Whitmore Hickman is a prolific author, having written numerous books for children as well as for adults. Among her many titles for adults are *I Will Not Leave You Desolate, Waiting and Loving,* and *The Growing Season.* Her books for children include *Eeps, Creeps, It's My Room; When Andy's Father Went to Prison;* and *My Friend William Moved Away.*

A native of Massachusetts, Ms. Hickman has resided in the South for many years. To her writing she brings the broad perspective of being a wife, mother, and grandmother; a professional woman; and a world traveler.

Of the writing of *Fullness of Time* Ms. Hickman says, "I like to travel, swim regularly, feel (so far!) no impingements of aging, but one wonders when that will begin to happen—and how will I handle it? Perhaps writing these stories is a way of preparing myself, testing scenarios, hoping that the faith and community that have seen me through some tough times will be with me till the end."